Math Practice: Grades 1–2

W9-BNM-691

Table of Contents

ISBN 978-1-60418-268-2

03-254121151

Ready-to-Use Ideas and Activities

The only way students truly will be able to manipulate numbers and have access to higher-level math concepts is to memorize the basic tables and understand fundamental concepts, such as counting, addition, subtraction, and multiplication.

The following activities can help to reinforce basic skills. These activities include a multi-sensory approach to helping students understand the concepts being introduced.

- Place a container filled with plastic discs near students' workspace. Plastic discs make great counters, which are extremely beneficial in helping students visualize mathematical concepts.

- Cut apart the flash cards provided in the back of this book. Starting with a flash card that shows small numbers, put a flash card on a flat surface. Use the discs and the equation signs to show what is on the flash card. For example:

- Use the discs to show $3 + 2 = 5$. After discs are in place, have students state the problem and the answer out loud. Students can also do this in small groups.

- Use the discs to show examples of addition, subtraction, and multiplication problems. For multiplication problems, group the discs. For example, to show $2 \times 3 = 6$, lay out 2 groups of 3 discs each. Explain that when you make 2 groups of 3 discs, you have 6 discs total.

- After doing a number of examples using the flash cards, let students make up their own problems and show them visually using the discs.

CD-104318 • © Carson-Dellosa

Ready-to-Use Ideas and Activities

- Obtain a pair of dice and anything that can act as a three-minute timer (a timer, a stopwatch, a watch with a second hand, etc.), or decide upon a certain number of rounds of play. Have each student roll the dice and add the numbers showing on the faces. Each correct answer is worth one point. The student with the most correct answers after a specific period of time or number of rounds wins. For example, a game may consist of six rounds. The student with the most points after six rounds wins. Alternately, the game can be played with subtraction, subtracting the smaller number from the larger.

- As players memorize answers and gain confidence, add additional dice. When using more than two dice, have players state the problem out loud and answer as they go. For instance, if the dice show 3, 6, and 4, the player would say, "3 plus 6 is 9 and 9 plus 4 is 13."

- Create a bingo sheet with five rows and five columns of blank squares. Write *FREE* in the middle square. Make enough copies to give one to each student. Write the flash card problems on a chalkboard and have students choose 24 problems from the board to write in the empty spaces of their bingo cards.

- When students have finished filling out their bingo cards, make the flash cards into a deck. Call out the answers one at a time. If a student has a problem on his card that equals the called-out answer, he should make an X through the problem to cross it out. Allow only one problem per answer. The student who first crosses out five problems in a row—horizontally, vertically, or diagonally—wins the game when she shouts, "Bingo!"

- Play another fun version of this game by writing answers on the bingo sheet and calling out the problems. To extend the game, continue playing until a student crosses out all of the problems on his bingo sheet.

Sums to 6

Solve each problem.

Jump to It!

1. 5
    +1

2. 6
    +0

3. 2
    +3

4. 0
    +2

5. 2
    +1

6. 3
    +0

7. 1
    +2

8. 3
    +2

9. 3
    +0

10. 3
    +2

11. 1
    +3

12. 1
    +4

13. 1
    +5

14. 0
    +0

15. 2
    +4

16. 0
    +5

17. 2
    +2

18. 2
    +3

19. 3
    +3

20. 4
    +1

21. 1
    +1

22. 2
    +4

23. 0
    +6

24. 4
    +2

25. 5
    +0

26. 3
    +1

27. 1
    +1

Name _____ Date _____

Sums to 6

Solve each problem.

You Can Do It!

1. $2 + 4 =$ 2. $1 + 5 =$ 3. $2 + 3 =$

4. $0 + 0 =$ 5. $2 + 1 =$ 6. $1 + 1 =$

7. $3 + 1 =$ 8. $5 + 1 =$ 9. $4 + 1 =$

10. $0 + 2 =$ 11. $0 + 5 =$ 12. $2 + 2 =$

13. $5 + 1 =$ 14. $3 + 2 =$ 15. $4 + 0 =$

16. $1 + 4 =$ 17. $4 + 2 =$ 18. $0 + 4 =$

19. $2 + 2 =$ 20. $1 + 3 =$ 21. $3 + 0 =$

22. $6 + 0 =$ 23. $2 + 1 =$

24. $0 + 6 =$ 25. $1 + 2 =$

26. $0 + 3 =$ 27. $2 + 3 =$

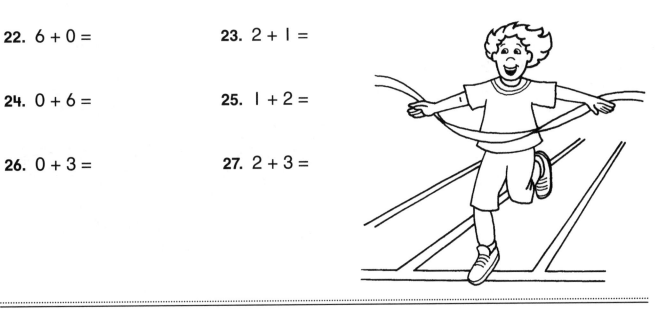

Sums to 7

Solve each problem.

Have Fun with Addition!

1. 2
   + 1

2. 1
   + 6

3. 4
   + 3

4. 6
   + 0

5. 5
   + 2

6. 7
   + 0

7. 2
   + 2

8. 2
   + 5

9. 2
   + 4

10. 3
   + 1

11. 1
   + 2

12. 3
   + 2

13. 4
   + 2

14. 3
   + 3

15. 5
   + 0

16. 0
   + 5

17. 2
   + 0

18. 3
   + 4

19. 6
   + 1

20. 5
   + 1

21. 0
   + 0

22. 3
   + 4

23. 4
   + 1

24. 5
   + 1

25. 0
   + 7

26. 2
   + 3

27. 1
   + 5

Sums to 10

Solve each problem.

Fly High with Addition!

1. 3
   + 3

2. 7
   + 3

3. 0
   + 3

4. 6
   + 2

5. 0
   + 9

6. 3
   + 6

7. 8
   + 0

8. 1
   + 4

9. 1
   + 8

10. 2
    + 5

11. 5
    + 5

12. 2
    + 3

13. 5
    + 1

14. 6
    + 1

15. 3
    + 5

16. 2
    + 7

17. 5
    + 4

18. 5
    + 2

19. 2
    + 8

20. 5
    + 3

21. 1
    + 2

22. 4
    + 4

23. 2
    + 2

24. 10
    + 0

25. 9
    + 1

26. 5
    + 0

27. 6
    + 4

Sums to 10

Solve each problem.

Total Problems: **27**
Problems Correct: _____

Practice Makes Perfect!

1. $\begin{array}{r} 7 \\ +\,2 \\ \hline \end{array}$
   2. $\begin{array}{r} 5 \\ +\,5 \\ \hline \end{array}$
   3. $\begin{array}{r} 2 \\ +\,6 \\ \hline \end{array}$
   4. $\begin{array}{r} 2 \\ +\,5 \\ \hline \end{array}$
   5. $\begin{array}{r} 5 \\ +\,0 \\ \hline \end{array}$
   6. $\begin{array}{r} 3 \\ +\,6 \\ \hline \end{array}$

7. $\begin{array}{r} 2 \\ +\,8 \\ \hline \end{array}$
   8. $\begin{array}{r} 9 \\ +\,1 \\ \hline \end{array}$
   9. $\begin{array}{r} 4 \\ +\,3 \\ \hline \end{array}$
   10. $\begin{array}{r} 4 \\ +\,5 \\ \hline \end{array}$
   11. $\begin{array}{r} 3 \\ +\,3 \\ \hline \end{array}$
   12. $\begin{array}{r} 5 \\ +\,4 \\ \hline \end{array}$

13. $\begin{array}{r} 6 \\ +\,1 \\ \hline \end{array}$
   14. $\begin{array}{r} 3 \\ +\,1 \\ \hline \end{array}$
   15. $\begin{array}{r} 2 \\ +\,2 \\ \hline \end{array}$
   16. $\begin{array}{r} 2 \\ +\,7 \\ \hline \end{array}$
   17. $\begin{array}{r} 3 \\ +\,5 \\ \hline \end{array}$
   18. $\begin{array}{r} 3 \\ +\,7 \\ \hline \end{array}$

19. $\begin{array}{r} 1 \\ +\,7 \\ \hline \end{array}$
   20. $\begin{array}{r} 4 \\ +\,2 \\ \hline \end{array}$
   21. $\begin{array}{r} 3 \\ +\,2 \\ \hline \end{array}$
   22. $\begin{array}{r} 1 \\ +\,0 \\ \hline \end{array}$
   23. $\begin{array}{r} 5 \\ +\,1 \\ \hline \end{array}$
   24. $\begin{array}{r} 1 \\ +\,1 \\ \hline \end{array}$

25. $\begin{array}{r} 8 \\ +\,1 \\ \hline \end{array}$
   26. $\begin{array}{r} 0 \\ +\,7 \\ \hline \end{array}$
   27. $\begin{array}{r} 6 \\ +\,2 \\ \hline \end{array}$

CD-104318 • © Carson-Dellosa

Sums to 10

Total Problems: 27
Problems Correct: _____

Solve each problem.

Way to Give a Royal Effort!

1. $1 + 6 =$

2. $0 + 1 =$

3. $4 + 5 =$

4. $4 + 2 =$

5. $3 + 6 =$

6. $1 + 3 =$

7. $7 + 2 =$

8. $3 + 2 =$

9. $8 + 2 =$

10. $4 + 3 =$

11. $6 + 3 =$

12. $5 + 3 =$

13. $1 + 3 =$

14. $4 + 6 =$

15. $2 + 0 =$

16. $5 + 1 =$

17. $5 + 2 =$

18. $6 + 4 =$

19. $5 + 5 =$

20. $2 + 1 =$

21. $2 + 6 =$

22. $4 + 1 =$

23. $0 + 4 =$

24. $0 + 4 =$

25. $6 + 2 =$

26. $9 + 0 =$

27. $2 + 8 =$

Name _____   Date _____

Differences from 6 or Less

Solve each problem.

Sss-ubtracting!

1. 6 −0	2. 4 −1	3. 0 −0	4. 6 −3	5. 6 −5	6. 3 −3
7. 6 −5	8. 4 −3	9. 4 −1	10. 6 −4	11. 5 −0	12. 4 −0
13. 5 −0	14. 5 −1	15. 4 −2	16. 0 −0	17. 2 −1	18. 3 −2
19. 1 −1	20. 2 −0	21. 6 −1	22. 5 −5	23. 5 −4	24. 6 −3
25. 4 −4	26. 6 −6	27. 5 −4			

Differences from 6 or Less

Solve each problem.

Discover the Answers!

1. $6 - 5 =$

2. $5 - 4 =$

3. $1 - 0 =$

4. $2 - 2 =$

5. $1 - 1 =$

6. $6 - 2 =$

7. $5 - 3 =$

8. $3 - 2 =$

9. $6 - 2 =$

10. $3 - 1 =$

11. $6 - 6 =$

12. $4 - 4 =$

13. $2 - 0 =$

14. $4 - 3 =$

15. $6 - 0 =$

16. $2 - 0 =$

17. $5 - 0 =$

18. $5 - 5 =$

19. $6 - 3 =$

20. $5 - 1 =$

21. $6 - 4 =$

22. $6 - 3 =$

23. $5 - 2 =$

24. $3 - 0 =$

25. $5 - 2 =$

26. $3 - 1 =$

27. $4 - 1 =$

Differences from 7 or Less

Solve each problem.

Busy as a Bee!

1. $\begin{array}{r} 5 \\ -2 \\ \hline \end{array}$
2. $\begin{array}{r} 6 \\ -2 \\ \hline \end{array}$
3. $\begin{array}{r} 0 \\ -0 \\ \hline \end{array}$
4. $\begin{array}{r} 7 \\ -2 \\ \hline \end{array}$
5. $\begin{array}{r} 6 \\ -4 \\ \hline \end{array}$
6. $\begin{array}{r} 2 \\ -1 \\ \hline \end{array}$

7. $\begin{array}{r} 7 \\ -4 \\ \hline \end{array}$
8. $\begin{array}{r} 7 \\ -3 \\ \hline \end{array}$
9. $\begin{array}{r} 4 \\ -4 \\ \hline \end{array}$
10. $\begin{array}{r} 3 \\ -2 \\ \hline \end{array}$
11. $\begin{array}{r} 6 \\ -1 \\ \hline \end{array}$
12. $\begin{array}{r} 4 \\ -1 \\ \hline \end{array}$

13. $\begin{array}{r} 7 \\ -5 \\ \hline \end{array}$
14. $\begin{array}{r} 3 \\ -0 \\ \hline \end{array}$
15. $\begin{array}{r} 6 \\ -3 \\ \hline \end{array}$
16. $\begin{array}{r} 5 \\ -3 \\ \hline \end{array}$
17. $\begin{array}{r} 7 \\ -5 \\ \hline \end{array}$
18. $\begin{array}{r} 4 \\ -2 \\ \hline \end{array}$

19. $\begin{array}{r} 5 \\ -4 \\ \hline \end{array}$
20. $\begin{array}{r} 6 \\ -5 \\ \hline \end{array}$
21. $\begin{array}{r} 7 \\ -6 \\ \hline \end{array}$
22. $\begin{array}{r} 7 \\ -0 \\ \hline \end{array}$
23. $\begin{array}{r} 7 \\ -2 \\ \hline \end{array}$
24. $\begin{array}{r} 5 \\ -0 \\ \hline \end{array}$

25. $\begin{array}{r} 3 \\ -3 \\ \hline \end{array}$
26. $\begin{array}{r} 7 \\ -1 \\ \hline \end{array}$
27. $\begin{array}{r} 7 \\ -4 \\ \hline \end{array}$

Differences from 7 or Less

Solve each problem.

Hard at Work!

1. $6 - 4 =$

2. $4 - 4 =$

3. $7 - 2 =$

4. $3 - 2 =$

5. $7 - 2 =$

6. $7 - 3 =$

7. $2 - 2 =$

8. $6 - 3 =$

9. $7 - 0 =$

10. $7 - 4 =$

11. $7 - 1 =$

12. $3 - 0 =$

13. $3 - 3 =$

14. $5 - 0 =$

15. $2 - 2 =$

16. $8 - 4 =$

17. $6 - 5 =$

18. $4 - 0 =$

19. $5 - 2 =$

20. $5 - 0 =$

21. $5 - 1 =$

22. $6 - 4 =$

23. $4 - 3 =$

24. $3 - 2 =$

25. $6 - 2 =$

26. $0 - 0 =$

27. $7 - 6 =$

Differences from 8 or Less

Solve each problem.

You're Doing Grrr-eat!

1. $\begin{array}{r} 6 \\ -2 \\ \hline \end{array}$ 2. $\begin{array}{r} 6 \\ -5 \\ \hline \end{array}$ 3. $\begin{array}{r} 8 \\ -3 \\ \hline \end{array}$ 4. $\begin{array}{r} 5 \\ -3 \\ \hline \end{array}$ 5. $\begin{array}{r} 7 \\ -7 \\ \hline \end{array}$ 6. $\begin{array}{r} 6 \\ -3 \\ \hline \end{array}$

7. $\begin{array}{r} 6 \\ -4 \\ \hline \end{array}$ 8. $\begin{array}{r} 8 \\ -7 \\ \hline \end{array}$ 9. $\begin{array}{r} 7 \\ -4 \\ \hline \end{array}$ 10. $\begin{array}{r} 8 \\ -6 \\ \hline \end{array}$ 11. $\begin{array}{r} 7 \\ -1 \\ \hline \end{array}$ 12. $\begin{array}{r} 7 \\ -6 \\ \hline \end{array}$

13. $\begin{array}{r} 8 \\ -1 \\ \hline \end{array}$ 14. $\begin{array}{r} 5 \\ -4 \\ \hline \end{array}$ 15. $\begin{array}{r} 5 \\ -2 \\ \hline \end{array}$ 16. $\begin{array}{r} 4 \\ -2 \\ \hline \end{array}$ 17. $\begin{array}{r} 6 \\ -0 \\ \hline \end{array}$ 18. $\begin{array}{r} 4 \\ -2 \\ \hline \end{array}$

19. $\begin{array}{r} 8 \\ -0 \\ \hline \end{array}$ 20. $\begin{array}{r} 6 \\ -6 \\ \hline \end{array}$ 21. $\begin{array}{r} 7 \\ -2 \\ \hline \end{array}$ 22. $\begin{array}{r} 8 \\ -2 \\ \hline \end{array}$ 23. $\begin{array}{r} 8 \\ -5 \\ \hline \end{array}$ 24. $\begin{array}{r} 8 \\ -4 \\ \hline \end{array}$

25. $\begin{array}{r} 5 \\ -5 \\ \hline \end{array}$ 26. $\begin{array}{r} 8 \\ -5 \\ \hline \end{array}$ 27. $\begin{array}{r} 8 \\ -4 \\ \hline \end{array}$

Differences from 8 or Less

Solve each problem.

Keep It Up!

1. $7 - 0 =$

2. $4 - 2 =$

3. $8 - 2 =$

4. $8 - 3 =$

5. $8 - 0 =$

6. $7 - 3 =$

7. $8 - 5 =$

8. $2 - 2 =$

9. $6 - 4 =$

10. $5 - 0 =$

11. $5 - 3 =$

12. $6 - 6 =$

13. $5 - 4 =$

14. $7 - 3 =$

15. $6 - 3 =$

16. $8 - 4 =$

17. $6 - 4 =$

18. $7 - 2 =$

19. $8 - 3 =$

20. $7 - 6 =$

21. $3 - 3 =$

22. $8 - 7 =$

23. $7 - 4 =$

24. $8 - 6 =$

25. $7 - 1 =$

26. $5 - 5 =$

27. $7 - 6 =$

Name _____   Date _____

Differences from 9 or Less

Solve each problem.

Up, Up, and Away with Subtracting!

1. 9
   − 3
   ____

2. 9
   − 5
   ____

3. 7
   − 3
   ____

4. 8
   − 5
   ____

5. 8
   − 2
   ____

6. 9
   − 6
   ____

7. 9
   − 2
   ____

8. 8
   − 1
   ____

9. 7
   − 5
   ____

10. 7
   − 2
   ____

11. 6
   − 5
   ____

12. 9
   − 9
   ____

13. 8
   − 8
   ____

14. 8
   − 6
   ____

15. 5
   − 4
   ____

16. 6
   − 2
   ____

17. 7
   − 6
   ____

18. 9
   − 4
   ____

19. 9
   − 0
   ____

20. 8
   − 3
   ____

21. 7
   − 1
   ____

22. 9
   − 6
   ____

23. 5
   − 3
   ____

24. 7
   − 4
   ____

25. 9
   − 1
   ____

26. 8
   − 4
   ____

27. 9
   − 8
   ____

Differences from 9 or Less

Solve each problem.

Stretch Your Brain!

1. $7 - 4 =$

2. $9 - 6 =$

3. $8 - 8 =$

4. $8 - 3 =$

5. $7 - 0 =$

6. $4 - 4 =$

7. $8 - 1 =$

8. $9 - 2 =$

9. $9 - 5 =$

10. $7 - 5 =$

11. $8 - 2 =$

12. $9 - 3 =$

13. $7 - 3 =$

14. $9 - 0 =$

15. $9 - 1 =$

16. $8 - 4 =$

17. $6 - 5 =$

18. $5 - 4 =$

19. $8 - 3 =$

20. $9 - 9 =$

21. $5 - 3 =$

22. $9 - 4 =$

23. $7 - 2 =$

24. $8 - 6 =$

25. $9 - 2 =$

26. $6 - 2 =$

27. $7 - 6 =$

Sums to 11

Solve each problem.

Away We Go with Addition!

1. $\begin{array}{r} 5 \\ +5 \\ \hline \end{array}$
2. $\begin{array}{r} 9 \\ +2 \\ \hline \end{array}$
3. $\begin{array}{r} 3 \\ +3 \\ \hline \end{array}$
4. $\begin{array}{r} 7 \\ +2 \\ \hline \end{array}$
5. $\begin{array}{r} 6 \\ +5 \\ \hline \end{array}$
6. $\begin{array}{r} 7 \\ +3 \\ \hline \end{array}$

7. $\begin{array}{r} 6 \\ +3 \\ \hline \end{array}$
8. $\begin{array}{r} 2 \\ +2 \\ \hline \end{array}$
9. $\begin{array}{r} 8 \\ +2 \\ \hline \end{array}$
10. $\begin{array}{r} 10 \\ +1 \\ \hline \end{array}$
11. $\begin{array}{r} 4 \\ +6 \\ \hline \end{array}$
12. $\begin{array}{r} 0 \\ +8 \\ \hline \end{array}$

13. $\begin{array}{r} 4 \\ +7 \\ \hline \end{array}$
14. $\begin{array}{r} 10 \\ +1 \\ \hline \end{array}$
15. $\begin{array}{r} 4 \\ +4 \\ \hline \end{array}$
16. $\begin{array}{r} 6 \\ +2 \\ \hline \end{array}$
17. $\begin{array}{r} 4 \\ +7 \\ \hline \end{array}$
18. $\begin{array}{r} 7 \\ +1 \\ \hline \end{array}$

19. $\begin{array}{r} 4 \\ +3 \\ \hline \end{array}$
20. $\begin{array}{r} 8 \\ +3 \\ \hline \end{array}$
21. $\begin{array}{r} 9 \\ +1 \\ \hline \end{array}$
22. $\begin{array}{r} 8 \\ +2 \\ \hline \end{array}$
23. $\begin{array}{r} 8 \\ +1 \\ \hline \end{array}$
24. $\begin{array}{r} 9 \\ +0 \\ \hline \end{array}$

25. $\begin{array}{r} 5 \\ +6 \\ \hline \end{array}$
26. $\begin{array}{r} 3 \\ +5 \\ \hline \end{array}$
27. $\begin{array}{r} 6 \\ +5 \\ \hline \end{array}$

Name _____   Date _____

Sums to 11

Total Problems: **27**
Problems Correct: _____

Solve each problem.

Reach High!

1. $5 + 5 =$

2. $7 + 2 =$

3. $6 + 4 =$

4. $5 + 2 =$

5. $9 + 1 =$

6. $6 + 2 =$

7. $2 + 2 =$

8. $7 + 4 =$

9. $4 + 4 =$

10. $8 + 3 =$

11. $6 + 3 =$

12. $2 + 4 =$

13. $10 + 1 =$

14. $0 + 6 =$

15. $2 + 5 =$

16. $8 + 1 =$

17. $5 + 1 =$

18. $6 + 1 =$

19. $2 + 3 =$

20. $8 + 0 =$

21. $1 + 10 =$

22. $7 + 3 =$

23. $4 + 1 =$

24. $8 + 2 =$

25. $7 + 0 =$

26. $5 + 4 =$

27. $3 + 4 =$

Sums to 12

Solve each problem.

Addition Is Cool!

1. $6 + 3 =$

2. $7 + 3 =$

3. $5 + 5 =$

4. $8 + 2 =$

5. $8 + 3 =$

6. $10 + 1 =$

7. $5 + 3 =$

8. $3 + 4 =$

9. $6 + 6 =$

10. $3 + 3 =$

11. $9 + 0 =$

12. $7 + 3 =$

13. $9 + 3 =$

14. $9 + 2 =$

15. $5 + 4 =$

16. $10 + 2 =$

17. $0 + 9 =$

18. $8 + 4 =$

19. $4 + 4 =$

20. $7 + 5 =$

21. $3 + 8 =$

22. $11 + 1 =$

23. $3 + 7 =$

24. $7 + 2 =$

25. $6 + 2 =$

26. $5 + 6 =$

27. $10 + 1 =$

Sums to 13

Solve each problem.

Spread Your Wings!

1. $5 + 4 =$

2. $10 + 3 =$

3. $7 + 3 =$

4. $8 + 4 =$

5. $7 + 5 =$

6. $5 + 8 =$

7. $6 + 3 =$

8. $5 + 5 =$

9. $7 + 2 =$

10. $7 + 4 =$

11. $12 + 1 =$

12. $10 + 2 =$

13. $11 + 1 =$

14. $4 + 9 =$

15. $8 + 2 =$

16. $10 + 1 =$

17. $3 + 10 =$

18. $6 + 6 =$

19. $8 + 3 =$

20. $3 + 9 =$

21. $9 + 4 =$

22. $8 + 0 =$

23. $2 + 5 =$

24. $7 + 0 =$

25. $9 + 3 =$

26. $9 + 2 =$

27. $6 + 7 =$

Sums to 13

Solve each problem.

Climb High with Addition!

1. 8
   + 4

2. 11
   + 2

3. 6
   + 5

4. 7
   + 6

5. 10
   + 3

6. 9
   + 4

7. 7
   + 2

8. 10
   + 2

9. 7
   + 3

10. 8
    + 2

11. 5
    + 3

12. 7
    + 4

13. 6
    + 5

14. 1
    + 0

15. 4
    + 4

16. 6
    + 5

17. 3
    + 4

18. 7
    + 6

19. 5
    + 4

20. 11
    + 2

21. 5
    + 5

22. 9
    + 2

23. 6
    + 3

24. 9
    + 3

25. 8
    + 5

26. 6
    + 4

27. 11
    + 1

Sums to 14

Solve each problem.

Keep Chugging Along!

1. 9
    + 4

2. 3
    + 7

3. 6
    + 4

4. 9
    + 2

5. 6
    + 6

6. 8
    + 6

7. 10
    + 4

8. 8
    + 3

9. 7
    + 4

10. 7
    + 6

11. 5
    + 2

12. 9
    + 3

13. 4
    + 5

14. 5
    + 5

15. 3
    + 4

16. 4
    + 9

17. 11
    + 3

18. 6
    + 8

19. 5
    + 9

20. 9
    + 5

21. 7
    + 5

22. 7
    + 6

23. 9
    + 1

24. 8
    + 5

25. 7
    + 7

26. 12
    + 2

27. 8
    + 1

Sums to 14

Solve each problem.

You're Doing Swimmingly!

1. $\begin{array}{r} 8 \\ +\ 3 \\ \hline \end{array}$
2. $\begin{array}{r} 9 \\ +\ 5 \\ \hline \end{array}$
3. $\begin{array}{r} 3 \\ +\ 8 \\ \hline \end{array}$
4. $\begin{array}{r} 2 \\ +\ 9 \\ \hline \end{array}$
5. $\begin{array}{r} 6 \\ +\ 8 \\ \hline \end{array}$
6. $\begin{array}{r} 7 \\ +\ 5 \\ \hline \end{array}$

7. $\begin{array}{r} 1 \\ +\ 9 \\ \hline \end{array}$
8. $\begin{array}{r} 8 \\ +\ 5 \\ \hline \end{array}$
9. $\begin{array}{r} 13 \\ +\ 1 \\ \hline \end{array}$
10. $\begin{array}{r} 7 \\ +\ 3 \\ \hline \end{array}$
11. $\begin{array}{r} 6 \\ +\ 5 \\ \hline \end{array}$
12. $\begin{array}{r} 4 \\ +\ 9 \\ \hline \end{array}$

13. $\begin{array}{r} 4 \\ +\ 6 \\ \hline \end{array}$
14. $\begin{array}{r} 9 \\ +\ 3 \\ \hline \end{array}$
15. $\begin{array}{r} 8 \\ +\ 2 \\ \hline \end{array}$
16. $\begin{array}{r} 7 \\ +\ 7 \\ \hline \end{array}$
17. $\begin{array}{r} 5 \\ +\ 8 \\ \hline \end{array}$
18. $\begin{array}{r} 4 \\ +\ 8 \\ \hline \end{array}$

19. $\begin{array}{r} 8 \\ +\ 4 \\ \hline \end{array}$
20. $\begin{array}{r} 5 \\ +\ 9 \\ \hline \end{array}$
21. $\begin{array}{r} 5 \\ +\ 7 \\ \hline \end{array}$
22. $\begin{array}{r} 10 \\ +\ 4 \\ \hline \end{array}$
23. $\begin{array}{r} 5 \\ +\ 6 \\ \hline \end{array}$
24. $\begin{array}{r} 4 \\ +\ 7 \\ \hline \end{array}$

25. $\begin{array}{r} 5 \\ +\ 5 \\ \hline \end{array}$
26. $\begin{array}{r} 12 \\ +\ 1 \\ \hline \end{array}$
27. $\begin{array}{r} 9 \\ +\ 5 \\ \hline \end{array}$

Sums to 14

Solve each problem.

Remember Your Addition!

1. 8
   +2

2. 10
   + 4

3. 2
   +9

4. 9
   +1

5. 4
   +9

6. 5
   +7

7. 6
   +6

8. 8
   +3

9. 9
   +5

10. 7
    +5

11. 7
    +6

12. 11
    + 0

13. 5
    +9

14. 3
    +8

15. 4
    +8

16. 3
    +7

17. 8
    +4

18. 6
    +5

19. 5
    +8

20. 3
    +9

21. 8
    +5

22. 9
    +4

23. 6
    +8

24. 6
    +7

25. 4
    +7

26. 5
    +6

27. 10
    + 0

Sums from 10 to 14

Solve each problem.

Moo-ving Right Along!

1. $8 + 4 =$

2. $13 + 1 =$

3. $7 + 7 =$

4. $9 + 5 =$

5. $14 + 0 =$

6. $2 + 9 =$

7. $6 + 8 =$

8. $6 + 5 =$

9. $9 + 3 =$

10. $1 + 9 =$

11. $4 + 7 =$

12. $5 + 8 =$

13. $4 + 8 =$

14. $8 + 3 =$

15. $10 + 2 =$

16. $6 + 6 =$

17. $7 + 3 =$

18. $7 + 4 =$

19. $7 + 5 =$

20. $7 + 6 =$

21. $9 + 2 =$

22. $2 + 8 =$

23. $5 + 9 =$

24. $3 + 7 =$

25. $5 + 6 =$

26. $3 + 8 =$

27. $9 + 4 =$

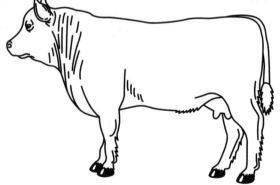

Name _____   Date _____

Sums to 15

Solve each problem.

Give It Your All!

1. 8 +4	2. 7 +5	3. 10 + 5
4. 7 +8	5. 5 +6	6. 7 +6

7. 9 +2	8. 6 +3	9. 4 +5
10. 8 +6	11. 7 +3	12. 6 +6

13. 9 +5	14. 9 +1	15. 8 +3
16. 5 +5	17. 9 +4	18. 8 +2

19. 6 +9	20. 8 +7	21. 8 +5
22. 11 + 2	23. 9 +3	24. 7 +4

25. 9 +6	26. 6 +7	27. 3 +8

Sums to 16

Solve each problem.

Mighty Math!

1. $\begin{array}{r}7\\+7\\\hline\end{array}$	2. $\begin{array}{r}6\\+6\\\hline\end{array}$	3. $\begin{array}{r}9\\+3\\\hline\end{array}$	4. $\begin{array}{r}9\\+6\\\hline\end{array}$	5. $\begin{array}{r}6\\+5\\\hline\end{array}$	6. $\begin{array}{r}12\\+4\\\hline\end{array}$
7. $\begin{array}{r}9\\+7\\\hline\end{array}$	8. $\begin{array}{r}7\\+3\\\hline\end{array}$	9. $\begin{array}{r}8\\+3\\\hline\end{array}$	10. $\begin{array}{r}6\\+7\\\hline\end{array}$	11. $\begin{array}{r}8\\+8\\\hline\end{array}$	12. $\begin{array}{r}7\\+5\\\hline\end{array}$
13. $\begin{array}{r}6\\+2\\\hline\end{array}$	14. $\begin{array}{r}7\\+6\\\hline\end{array}$	15. $\begin{array}{r}9\\+2\\\hline\end{array}$	16. $\begin{array}{r}7\\+8\\\hline\end{array}$	17. $\begin{array}{r}15\\+1\\\hline\end{array}$	18. $\begin{array}{r}9\\+4\\\hline\end{array}$
19. $\begin{array}{r}9\\+5\\\hline\end{array}$	20. $\begin{array}{r}8\\+4\\\hline\end{array}$	21. $\begin{array}{r}5\\+5\\\hline\end{array}$	22. $\begin{array}{r}8\\+3\\\hline\end{array}$	23. $\begin{array}{r}7\\+2\\\hline\end{array}$	24. $\begin{array}{r}8\\+2\\\hline\end{array}$
25. $\begin{array}{r}6\\+4\\\hline\end{array}$	26. $\begin{array}{r}11\\+4\\\hline\end{array}$	27. $\begin{array}{r}9\\+1\\\hline\end{array}$			

Name _____ Date _____

Sums to 17

Solve each problem.

Spring into Addition!

1. 8
   + 2
   ___

2. 9
   + 8
   ___

3. 6
   + 4
   ___

4. 9
   + 6
   ___

5. 6
   + 5
   ___

6. 8
   + 8
   ___

7. 7
   + 6
   ___

8. 15
   + 2
   ___

9. 9
   + 2
   ___

10. 7
    + 5
    ___

11. 5
    + 5
    ___

12. 5
    + 6
    ___

13. 7
    + 4
    ___

14. 6
    + 6
    ___

15. 8
    + 6
    ___

16. 7
    + 8
    ___

17. 9
    + 4
    ___

18. 8
    + 7
    ___

19. 8
    + 6
    ___

20. 8
    + 9
    ___

21. 9
    + 1
    ___

22. 7
    + 3
    ___

23. 9
    + 3
    ___

24. 11
    + 6
    ___

25. 10
    + 7
    ___

26. 7
    + 2
    ___

27. 5
    + 8
    ___

Sums to 18

Solve each problem.

Addition Is a Blast!

1. 9
    $+6$

2. 10
    $+\ 8$

3. 8
    $+5$

4. 6
    $+7$

5. 5
    $+5$

6. 6
    $+4$

7. 9
    $+7$

8. 12
    $+\ 6$

9. 5
    $+6$

10. 9
    $+9$

11. 6
    $+3$

12. 7
    $+4$

13. 8
    $+6$

14. 7
    $+6$

15. 7
    $+5$

16. 9
    $+5$

17. 8
    $+7$

18. 9
    $+3$

19. 8
    $+2$

20. 9
    $+4$

21. 8
    $+8$

22. 11
    $+\ 3$

23. 8
    $+3$

24. 9
    $+8$

25. 6
    $+6$

26. 7
    $+3$

27. 9
    $+9$

Name _____ Date _____

Sums to 18

Solve each problem.

You're a Math Superstar!

1. $7 + 5 =$ 2. $5 + 9 =$ 3. $8 + 4 =$

4. $5 + 3 =$ 5. $9 + 5 =$ 6. $8 + 8 =$

7. $3 + 7 =$ 8. $10 + 3 =$ 9. $11 + 7 =$

10. $9 + 2 =$ 11. $6 + 4 =$ 12. $6 + 7 =$

13. $7 + 8 =$ 14. $9 + 3 =$ 15. $2 + 9 =$

16. $7 + 9 =$ 17. $7 + 2 =$ 18. $3 + 8 =$

19. $4 + 6 =$ 20. $11 + 2 =$ 21. $2 + 4 =$

22. $3 + 2 =$ 23. $8 + 9 =$

24. $4 + 0 =$ 25. $4 + 9 =$

26. $16 + 0 =$ 27. $4 + 7 =$

Sums from 10 to 18

Solve each problem.

Slide into Addition!

1. 7
  + 6

2. 2
  + 9

3. 4
  + 8

4. 6
  + 5

5. 9
  + 7

6. 9
  + 9

7. 6
  + 8

8. 5
  + 9

9. 8
  + 9

10. 3
  + 9

11. 7
  + 9

12. 9
  + 8

13. 8
  + 7

14. 6
  + 9

15. 8
  + 6

16. 9
  + 5

17. 10
  + 3

18. 7
  + 7

19. 4
  + 9

20. 5
  + 8

21. 16
  + 2

22. 8
  + 8

23. 6
  + 4

24. 7
  + 3

25. 9
  + 6

26. 5
  + 7

27. 7
  + 8

CD-104318 • © Carson-Dellosa

Sums from 10 to 18

Solve each problem.

Way to Go!

1. 8
   +9

2. 8
   +3

3. 7
   +9

4. 6
   +8

5. 7
   +6

6. 9
   +6

7. 6
   +9

8. 7
   +8

9. 11
   +0

10. 3
   +9

11. 8
   +4

12. 9
   +7

13. 7
   +7

14. 5
   +9

15. 8
   +6

16. 14
   +1

17. 9
   +4

18. 6
   +7

19. 2
   +8

20. 9
   +8

21. 6
   +6

22. 8
   +7

23. 7
   +5

24. 5
   +5

25. 9
   +9

26. 6
   +4

27. 10
   +2

1st PLACE

Sums from 10 to 18

Total Problems:	27
Problems Correct:	_____

Solve each problem.

Addition Is Your Friend!

1. $6 + 7 =$

2. $8 + 9 =$

3. $8 + 8 =$

4. $9 + 6 =$

5. $7 + 9 =$

6. $9 + 9 =$

7. $8 + 7 =$

8. $6 + 5 =$

9. $7 + 8 =$

10. $9 + 5 =$

11. $9 + 2 =$

12. $4 + 8 =$

13. $5 + 7 =$

14. $7 + 3 =$

15. $10 + 8 =$

16. $8 + 6 =$

17. $11 + 3 =$

18. $8 + 5 =$

19. $8 + 3 =$

20. $8 + 2 =$

21. $7 + 7 =$

22. $5 + 6 =$

23. $2 + 12 =$

24. $5 + 8 =$

25. $9 + 7 =$

26. $5 + 5 =$

27. $9 + 8 =$

Differences from 10 or Less

Solve each problem.

A Good Attitude Is Key!

1. $\begin{array}{r} 9 \\ -6 \\ \hline \end{array}$

2. $\begin{array}{r} 8 \\ -2 \\ \hline \end{array}$

3. $\begin{array}{r} 10 \\ -0 \\ \hline \end{array}$

4. $\begin{array}{r} 10 \\ -9 \\ \hline \end{array}$

5. $\begin{array}{r} 10 \\ -3 \\ \hline \end{array}$

6. $\begin{array}{r} 9 \\ -6 \\ \hline \end{array}$

7. $\begin{array}{r} 4 \\ -2 \\ \hline \end{array}$

8. $\begin{array}{r} 7 \\ -4 \\ \hline \end{array}$

9. $\begin{array}{r} 10 \\ -4 \\ \hline \end{array}$

10. $\begin{array}{r} 10 \\ -10 \\ \hline \end{array}$

11. $\begin{array}{r} 9 \\ -4 \\ \hline \end{array}$

12. $\begin{array}{r} 10 \\ -2 \\ \hline \end{array}$

13. $\begin{array}{r} 8 \\ -6 \\ \hline \end{array}$

14. $\begin{array}{r} 10 \\ -5 \\ \hline \end{array}$

15. $\begin{array}{r} 7 \\ -5 \\ \hline \end{array}$

16. $\begin{array}{r} 9 \\ -5 \\ \hline \end{array}$

17. $\begin{array}{r} 8 \\ -5 \\ \hline \end{array}$

18. $\begin{array}{r} 8 \\ -7 \\ \hline \end{array}$

19. $\begin{array}{r} 7 \\ -3 \\ \hline \end{array}$

20. $\begin{array}{r} 3 \\ -2 \\ \hline \end{array}$

21. $\begin{array}{r} 10 \\ -3 \\ \hline \end{array}$

22. $\begin{array}{r} 6 \\ -2 \\ \hline \end{array}$

23. $\begin{array}{r} 10 \\ -1 \\ \hline \end{array}$

24. $\begin{array}{r} 9 \\ -3 \\ \hline \end{array}$

25. $\begin{array}{r} 7 \\ -6 \\ \hline \end{array}$

26. $\begin{array}{r} 10 \\ -4 \\ \hline \end{array}$

27. $\begin{array}{r} 10 \\ -8 \\ \hline \end{array}$

Differences from 10 or Less

Solve each problem.

Hop to It!

1. $7 - 6 =$ 2. $10 - 5 =$ 3. $8 - 7 =$

4. $9 - 3 =$ 5. $9 - 1 =$ 6. $10 - 0 =$

7. $9 - 5 =$ 8. $8 - 2 =$ 9. $10 - 3 =$

10. $7 - 2 =$ 11. $10 - 1 =$ 12. $8 - 1 =$

13. $10 - 2 =$ 14. $8 - 6 =$ 15. $10 - 4 =$

16. $5 - 1 =$ 17. $3 - 1 =$ 18. $7 - 5 =$

19. $8 - 3 =$ 20. $6 - 5 =$ 21. $8 - 4 =$

22. $9 - 3 =$ 23. $6 - 0 =$

24. $0 - 0 =$ 25. $4 - 1 =$

26. $1 - 1 =$ 27. $9 - 2 =$

Name _____ Date _____

Differences from 10 or Less

Solve each problem.

Whale of a Job!

1. 9
  − 7

2. 10
  − 0

3. 6
  − 1

4. 10
  − 9

5. 10
  − 2

6. 7
  − 6

7. 1
  − 1

8. 4
  − 3

9. 4
  − 2

10. 8
  − 3

11. 8
  − 6

12. 10
  − 3

13. 6
  − 5

14. 7
  − 5

15. 7
  − 2

16. 5
  − 1

17. 1
  − 0

18. 10
  − 6

19. 9
  − 0

20. 10
  − 7

21. 8
  − 5

22. 6
  − 2

23. 6
  − 3

24. 9
  − 1

25. 9
  − 3

26. 3
  − 0

27. 9
  − 6

Differences from 10 or Less

Solve each problem.

Explore Subtracting!

1. $10 - 5 =$

2. $3 - 3 =$

3. $10 - 8 =$

4. $4 - 1 =$

5. $5 - 0 =$

6. $10 - 6 =$

7. $6 - 1 =$

8. $7 - 3 =$

9. $1 - 1 =$

10. $6 - 2 =$

11. $8 - 0 =$

12. $10 - 10 =$

13. $9 - 4 =$

14. $8 - 8 =$

15. $10 - 2 =$

16. $4 - 3 =$

17. $5 - 3 =$

18. $10 - 7 =$

19. $8 - 3 =$

20. $1 - 1 =$

21. $5 - 2 =$

22. $9 - 8 =$

23. $7 - 6 =$

24. $6 - 4 =$

25. $8 - 2 =$

26. $10 - 7 =$

27. $7 - 5 =$

Name _____ Date _____

Differences from 10 or Less

Solve each problem.

Tossing Numbers Around!

1. 9
   − 9
   ———

2. 10
   − 7
   ———

3. 10
   − 5
   ———

4. 9
   − 7
   ———

5. 6
   − 5
   ———

6. 3
   − 2
   ———

7. 9
   − 0
   ———

8. 6
   − 3
   ———

9. 10
   − 8
   ———

10. 1
   − 0
   ———

11. 5
   − 2
   ———

12. 5
   − 1
   ———

13. 10
   − 2
   ———

14. 6
   − 6
   ———

15. 4
   − 2
   ———

16. 3
   − 3
   ———

17. 8
   − 5
   ———

18. 3
   − 1
   ———

19. 9
   − 6
   ———

20. 8
   − 7
   ———

21. 6
   − 4
   ———

22. 2
   − 1
   ———

23. 5
   − 4
   ———

24. 1
   − 1
   ———

25. 5
   − 3
   ———

26. 8
   − 6
   ———

27. 10
   − 3
   ———

Differences from 11 or Less

Solve each problem.

Ace Subtraction!

1. $9 - 0 =$

2. $7 - 6 =$

3. $9 - 8 =$

4. $9 - 2 =$

5. $11 - 5 =$

6. $11 - 4 =$

7. $11 - 3 =$

8. $11 - 5 =$

9. $8 - 5 =$

10. $10 - 2 =$

11. $9 - 8 =$

12. $11 - 4 =$

13. $8 - 7 =$

14. $10 - 4 =$

15. $11 - 1 =$

16. $11 - 8 =$

17. $10 - 8 =$

18. $10 - 6 =$

19. $11 - 2 =$

20. $11 - 6 =$

21. $9 - 3 =$

22. $11 - 10 =$

23. $9 - 3 =$

24. $11 - 3 =$

25. $8 - 6 =$

26. $10 - 5 =$

27. $9 - 1 =$

Name _____   Date _____

Differences from 11 or Less

Total Problems: 27
Problems Correct: _____

Solve each problem.

Slow and Steady!

1. $\begin{array}{r} 9 \\ -\ 0 \\ \hline \end{array}$ 2. $\begin{array}{r} 11 \\ -\ 9 \\ \hline \end{array}$ 3. $\begin{array}{r} 11 \\ -\ 1 \\ \hline \end{array}$ 4. $\begin{array}{r} 11 \\ -\ 3 \\ \hline \end{array}$ 5. $\begin{array}{r} 7 \\ -\ 5 \\ \hline \end{array}$ 6. $\begin{array}{r} 9 \\ -\ 6 \\ \hline \end{array}$

7. $\begin{array}{r} 8 \\ -\ 6 \\ \hline \end{array}$ 8. $\begin{array}{r} 2 \\ -\ 7 \\ \hline \end{array}$ 9. $\begin{array}{r} 11 \\ -\ 4 \\ \hline \end{array}$ 10. $\begin{array}{r} 10 \\ -\ 8 \\ \hline \end{array}$ 11. $\begin{array}{r} 11 \\ -\ 3 \\ \hline \end{array}$ 12. $\begin{array}{r} 8 \\ -\ 7 \\ \hline \end{array}$

13. $\begin{array}{r} 11 \\ -\ 7 \\ \hline \end{array}$ 14. $\begin{array}{r} 10 \\ -\ 6 \\ \hline \end{array}$ 15. $\begin{array}{r} 11 \\ -\ 10 \\ \hline \end{array}$ 16. $\begin{array}{r} 9 \\ -\ 8 \\ \hline \end{array}$ 17. $\begin{array}{r} 11 \\ -\ 5 \\ \hline \end{array}$ 18. $\begin{array}{r} 9 \\ -\ 5 \\ \hline \end{array}$

19. $\begin{array}{r} 8 \\ -\ 5 \\ \hline \end{array}$ 20. $\begin{array}{r} 9 \\ -\ 2 \\ \hline \end{array}$ 21. $\begin{array}{r} 10 \\ -\ 7 \\ \hline \end{array}$ 22. $\begin{array}{r} 5 \\ -\ 2 \\ \hline \end{array}$ 23. $\begin{array}{r} 11 \\ -\ 5 \\ \hline \end{array}$ 24. $\begin{array}{r} 11 \\ -\ 2 \\ \hline \end{array}$

25. $\begin{array}{r} 10 \\ -\ 5 \\ \hline \end{array}$ 26. $\begin{array}{r} 11 \\ -\ 6 \\ \hline \end{array}$ 27. $\begin{array}{r} 8 \\ -\ 8 \\ \hline \end{array}$

Differences from 12 or Less

Solve each problem.

Total Problems: **27**
Problems Correct: _____

Monkey Around with Subtraction!

1. $11 - 5 =$

2. $10 - 3 =$

3. $12 - 5 =$

4. $9 - 3 =$

5. $11 - 7 =$

6. $12 - 2 =$

7. $8 - 5 =$

8. $12 - 6 =$

9. $11 - 9 =$

10. $12 - 4 =$

11. $10 - 3 =$

12. $11 - 9 =$

13. $10 - 2 =$

14. $12 - 8 =$

15. $12 - 3 =$

16. $8 - 6 =$

17. $12 - 12 =$

18. $9 - 2 =$

19. $8 - 1 =$

20. $10 - 6 =$

21. $12 - 1 =$

22. $11 - 8 =$

23. $10 - 7 =$

24. $8 - 6 =$

25. $11 - 4 =$

26. $10 - 9 =$

27. $12 - 9 =$

CD-104318 • © Carson-Dellosa

Differences from 12 or Less

Solve each problem.

Zooming Through Subtraction!

1. $11 - 5 =$ 2. $10 - 3 =$ 3. $12 - 5 =$

4. $9 - 3 =$ 5. $11 - 7 =$ 6. $12 - 2 =$

7. $8 - 5 =$ 8. $9 - 2 =$ 9. $11 - 9 =$

10. $12 - 4 =$ 11. $10 - 1 =$ 12. $12 - 9 =$

13. $10 - 4 =$ 14. $12 - 8 =$ 15. $10 - 2 =$

16. $8 - 4 =$ 17. $12 - 3 =$ 18. $12 - 6 =$

19. $8 - 3 =$ 20. $10 - 6 =$ 21. $12 - 1 =$

22. $11 - 8 =$ 23. $11 - 6 =$

24. $8 - 6 =$ 25. $11 - 4 =$

26. $10 - 7 =$ 27. $7 - 6 =$

Name _____ Date _____

Differences from 13 or Less

Solve each problem.

You're on the Right Track!

1. 11   2. 12   3. 10   4. 13   5. 10   6. 12
   − 5   − 4   − 5   − 4   − 9   − 4

7. 13   8. 10   9. 12   10. 12   11. 13   12. 12
   − 5   − 6   − 6   − 3   − 7   − 5

13. 13   14. 13   15. 12   16. 11   17. 10   18. 11
   − 8   − 9   − 4   − 6   − 4   − 8

19. 13   20. 12   21. 13   22. 10   23. 12   24. 12
   − 5   − 7   − 7   − 3   − 6   − 8

25. 12   26. 11   27. 10
   − 9   − 7   − 8

Name _____ Date _____

Differences from 14 or Less

Solve each problem.

Have a Ball Subtracting!

1. 12
    − 5

2. 13
    − 7

3. 12
    − 8

4. 13
    − 6

5. 13
    − 8

6. 10
    − 8

7. 14
    − 8

8. 10
    − 4

9. 14
    − 6

10. 13
    − 4

11. 12
    − 7

12. 11
    − 9

13. 13
    − 9

14. 14
    − 4

15. 14
    − 9

16. 12
    − 6

17. 13
    − 9

18. 14
    − 2

19. 14
    − 7

20. 14
    − 5

21. 10
    − 6

22. 14
    − 2

23. 11
    − 8

24. 12
    − 9

25. 13
    − 5

26. 11
    − 2

27. 11
    − 0

Differences from 14 or Less

Solve each problem.

Total Problems: **27**
Problems Correct: _____

Be a Fan of Subtraction!

1. $\begin{array}{r} 11 \\ -\ 8 \\ \hline \end{array}$
2. $\begin{array}{r} 7 \\ -\ 2 \\ \hline \end{array}$
3. $\begin{array}{r} 14 \\ -\ 8 \\ \hline \end{array}$
4. $\begin{array}{r} 13 \\ -\ 6 \\ \hline \end{array}$
5. $\begin{array}{r} 8 \\ -\ 3 \\ \hline \end{array}$
6. $\begin{array}{r} 10 \\ -\ 6 \\ \hline \end{array}$

7. $\begin{array}{r} 13 \\ -\ 9 \\ \hline \end{array}$
8. $\begin{array}{r} 12 \\ -\ 8 \\ \hline \end{array}$
9. $\begin{array}{r} 10 \\ -\ 9 \\ \hline \end{array}$
10. $\begin{array}{r} 10 \\ -\ 7 \\ \hline \end{array}$
11. $\begin{array}{r} 11 \\ -\ 4 \\ \hline \end{array}$
12. $\begin{array}{r} 14 \\ -\ 6 \\ \hline \end{array}$

13. $\begin{array}{r} 12 \\ -\ 6 \\ \hline \end{array}$
14. $\begin{array}{r} 13 \\ -\ 7 \\ \hline \end{array}$
15. $\begin{array}{r} 12 \\ -\ 9 \\ \hline \end{array}$
16. $\begin{array}{r} 11 \\ -\ 3 \\ \hline \end{array}$
17. $\begin{array}{r} 13 \\ -\ 4 \\ \hline \end{array}$
18. $\begin{array}{r} 11 \\ -\ 7 \\ \hline \end{array}$

19. $\begin{array}{r} 11 \\ -\ 5 \\ \hline \end{array}$
20. $\begin{array}{r} 10 \\ -\ 2 \\ \hline \end{array}$
21. $\begin{array}{r} 14 \\ -\ 5 \\ \hline \end{array}$
22. $\begin{array}{r} 12 \\ -\ 4 \\ \hline \end{array}$
23. $\begin{array}{r} 12 \\ -\ 5 \\ \hline \end{array}$
24. $\begin{array}{r} 13 \\ -\ 5 \\ \hline \end{array}$

25. $\begin{array}{r} 11 \\ -\ 7 \\ \hline \end{array}$
26. $\begin{array}{r} 12 \\ -\ 3 \\ \hline \end{array}$
27. $\begin{array}{r} 14 \\ -\ 9 \\ \hline \end{array}$

Differences from 14 or Less

Total Problems: 27
Problems Correct: _____

Solve each problem.

Get Jazzed About Subtraction!

1. $\begin{array}{r} 11 \\ -\ 2 \\ \hline \end{array}$ 2. $\begin{array}{r} 10 \\ -\ 5 \\ \hline \end{array}$ 3. $\begin{array}{r} 11 \\ -\ 3 \\ \hline \end{array}$ 4. $\begin{array}{r} 10 \\ -\ 3 \\ \hline \end{array}$ 5. $\begin{array}{r} 11 \\ -\ 6 \\ \hline \end{array}$ 6. $\begin{array}{r} 12 \\ -\ 9 \\ \hline \end{array}$

7. $\begin{array}{r} 10 \\ -\ 4 \\ \hline \end{array}$ 8. $\begin{array}{r} 6 \\ -\ 3 \\ \hline \end{array}$ 9. $\begin{array}{r} 14 \\ -\ 8 \\ \hline \end{array}$ 10. $\begin{array}{r} 12 \\ -\ 3 \\ \hline \end{array}$ 11. $\begin{array}{r} 12 \\ -\ 6 \\ \hline \end{array}$ 12. $\begin{array}{r} 11 \\ -\ 4 \\ \hline \end{array}$

13. $\begin{array}{r} 8 \\ -\ 4 \\ \hline \end{array}$ 14. $\begin{array}{r} 12 \\ -\ 5 \\ \hline \end{array}$ 15. $\begin{array}{r} 13 \\ -\ 4 \\ \hline \end{array}$ 16. $\begin{array}{r} 11 \\ -\ 5 \\ \hline \end{array}$ 17. $\begin{array}{r} 13 \\ -\ 8 \\ \hline \end{array}$ 18. $\begin{array}{r} 14 \\ -\ 5 \\ \hline \end{array}$

19. $\begin{array}{r} 12 \\ -\ 8 \\ \hline \end{array}$ 20. $\begin{array}{r} 14 \\ -\ 9 \\ \hline \end{array}$ 21. $\begin{array}{r} 13 \\ -\ 5 \\ \hline \end{array}$ 22. $\begin{array}{r} 12 \\ -\ 4 \\ \hline \end{array}$ 23. $\begin{array}{r} 13 \\ -\ 6 \\ \hline \end{array}$ 24. $\begin{array}{r} 9 \\ -\ 6 \\ \hline \end{array}$

25. $\begin{array}{r} 13 \\ -\ 9 \\ \hline \end{array}$ 26. $\begin{array}{r} 12 \\ -\ 7 \\ \hline \end{array}$ 27. $\begin{array}{r} 14 \\ -\ 7 \\ \hline \end{array}$

Differences from 14 or Less

Total Problems: **27**
Problems Correct: _____

Solve each problem.

You Can Do It!

1. $\begin{array}{r} 13 \\ -\ 6 \\ \hline \end{array}$
2. $\begin{array}{r} 10 \\ -\ 8 \\ \hline \end{array}$
3. $\begin{array}{r} 12 \\ -\ 8 \\ \hline \end{array}$
4. $\begin{array}{r} 13 \\ -\ 4 \\ \hline \end{array}$
5. $\begin{array}{r} 12 \\ -\ 4 \\ \hline \end{array}$
6. $\begin{array}{r} 13 \\ -\ 7 \\ \hline \end{array}$

7. $\begin{array}{r} 11 \\ -\ 7 \\ \hline \end{array}$
8. $\begin{array}{r} 14 \\ -\ 7 \\ \hline \end{array}$
9. $\begin{array}{r} 12 \\ -\ 3 \\ \hline \end{array}$
10. $\begin{array}{r} 9 \\ -\ 7 \\ \hline \end{array}$
11. $\begin{array}{r} 6 \\ -\ 2 \\ \hline \end{array}$
12. $\begin{array}{r} 11 \\ -\ 6 \\ \hline \end{array}$

13. $\begin{array}{r} 5 \\ -\ 3 \\ \hline \end{array}$
14. $\begin{array}{r} 11 \\ -\ 8 \\ \hline \end{array}$
15. $\begin{array}{r} 12 \\ -\ 6 \\ \hline \end{array}$
16. $\begin{array}{r} 10 \\ -\ 1 \\ \hline \end{array}$
17. $\begin{array}{r} 12 \\ -\ 5 \\ \hline \end{array}$
18. $\begin{array}{r} 12 \\ -\ 7 \\ \hline \end{array}$

19. $\begin{array}{r} 13 \\ -\ 5 \\ \hline \end{array}$
20. $\begin{array}{r} 13 \\ -\ 9 \\ \hline \end{array}$
21. $\begin{array}{r} 11 \\ -\ 2 \\ \hline \end{array}$
22. $\begin{array}{r} 13 \\ -\ 8 \\ \hline \end{array}$
23. $\begin{array}{r} 11 \\ -\ 3 \\ \hline \end{array}$
24. $\begin{array}{r} 8 \\ -\ 5 \\ \hline \end{array}$

25. $\begin{array}{r} 14 \\ -\ 8 \\ \hline \end{array}$
26. $\begin{array}{r} 11 \\ -\ 9 \\ \hline \end{array}$
27. $\begin{array}{r} 7 \\ -\ 4 \\ \hline \end{array}$

Name _____ Date _____

Differences from 15 or Less

Solve each problem.

Great Job!

1. $10 - 9$

2. $15 - 9$

3. $13 - 5$

4. $15 - 8$

5. $12 - 7$

6. $14 - 6$

7. $10 - 4$

8. $12 - 8$

9. $13 - 9$

10. $15 - 5$

11. $12 - 5$

12. $15 - 3$

13. $14 - 5$

14. $12 - 6$

15. $12 - 4$

16. $11 - 6$

17. $15 - 2$

18. $10 - 6$

19. $13 - 6$

20. $13 - 8$

21. $12 - 9$

22. $13 - 3$

23. $15 - 7$

24. $14 - 7$

25. $15 - 8$

26. $10 - 5$

27. $15 - 1$

Name _____   Date _____

Differences from 10 to 18

Total Problems: 27
Problems Correct: _____

Solve each problem.

Pace Yourself!

1. $\begin{array}{r} 13 \\ -\ 8 \\ \hline \end{array}$ 2. $\begin{array}{r} 15 \\ -\ 6 \\ \hline \end{array}$ 3. $\begin{array}{r} 17 \\ -\ 8 \\ \hline \end{array}$ 4. $\begin{array}{r} 16 \\ -\ 9 \\ \hline \end{array}$ 5. $\begin{array}{r} 18 \\ -\ 9 \\ \hline \end{array}$ 6. $\begin{array}{r} 14 \\ -\ 9 \\ \hline \end{array}$

7. $\begin{array}{r} 13 \\ -\ 9 \\ \hline \end{array}$ 8. $\begin{array}{r} 13 \\ -\ 6 \\ \hline \end{array}$ 9. $\begin{array}{r} 12 \\ -\ 6 \\ \hline \end{array}$ 10. $\begin{array}{r} 10 \\ -\ 3 \\ \hline \end{array}$ 11. $\begin{array}{r} 12 \\ -\ 9 \\ \hline \end{array}$ 12. $\begin{array}{r} 15 \\ -\ 9 \\ \hline \end{array}$

13. $\begin{array}{r} 15 \\ -\ 8 \\ \hline \end{array}$ 14. $\begin{array}{r} 11 \\ -\ 9 \\ \hline \end{array}$ 15. $\begin{array}{r} 15 \\ -\ 7 \\ \hline \end{array}$ 16. $\begin{array}{r} 11 \\ -\ 8 \\ \hline \end{array}$ 17. $\begin{array}{r} 16 \\ -\ 7 \\ \hline \end{array}$ 18. $\begin{array}{r} 10 \\ -\ 4 \\ \hline \end{array}$

19. $\begin{array}{r} 14 \\ -\ 5 \\ \hline \end{array}$ 20. $\begin{array}{r} 12 \\ -\ 7 \\ \hline \end{array}$ 21. $\begin{array}{r} 17 \\ -\ 9 \\ \hline \end{array}$ 22. $\begin{array}{r} 10 \\ -\ 3 \\ \hline \end{array}$ 23. $\begin{array}{r} 16 \\ -\ 8 \\ \hline \end{array}$ 24. $\begin{array}{r} 16 \\ -\ 9 \\ \hline \end{array}$

25. $\begin{array}{r} 12 \\ -\ 3 \\ \hline \end{array}$ 26. $\begin{array}{r} 14 \\ -\ 6 \\ \hline \end{array}$ 27. $\begin{array}{r} 11 \\ -\ 7 \\ \hline \end{array}$

          CD-104318 • © Carson-Dellosa

Name _____ Date _____

Differences from 10 to 18

Total Problems: **27**
Problems Correct: _____

Solve each problem.

Now You're Singing!

1. $\begin{array}{r} 10 \\ -\ 5 \\ \hline \end{array}$
2. $\begin{array}{r} 15 \\ -\ 6 \\ \hline \end{array}$
3. $\begin{array}{r} 12 \\ -\ 8 \\ \hline \end{array}$
4. $\begin{array}{r} 12 \\ -\ 6 \\ \hline \end{array}$
5. $\begin{array}{r} 13 \\ -\ 7 \\ \hline \end{array}$
6. $\begin{array}{r} 12 \\ -\ 5 \\ \hline \end{array}$

7. $\begin{array}{r} 17 \\ -\ 9 \\ \hline \end{array}$
8. $\begin{array}{r} 11 \\ -\ 8 \\ \hline \end{array}$
9. $\begin{array}{r} 11 \\ -\ 9 \\ \hline \end{array}$
10. $\begin{array}{r} 18 \\ -\ 9 \\ \hline \end{array}$
11. $\begin{array}{r} 14 \\ -\ 5 \\ \hline \end{array}$
12. $\begin{array}{r} 14 \\ -\ 9 \\ \hline \end{array}$

13. $\begin{array}{r} 14 \\ -\ 6 \\ \hline \end{array}$
14. $\begin{array}{r} 13 \\ -\ 9 \\ \hline \end{array}$
15. $\begin{array}{r} 14 \\ -\ 8 \\ \hline \end{array}$
16. $\begin{array}{r} 11 \\ -\ 3 \\ \hline \end{array}$
17. $\begin{array}{r} 16 \\ -\ 8 \\ \hline \end{array}$
18. $\begin{array}{r} 15 \\ -\ 8 \\ \hline \end{array}$

19. $\begin{array}{r} 10 \\ -\ 2 \\ \hline \end{array}$
20. $\begin{array}{r} 16 \\ -\ 7 \\ \hline \end{array}$
21. $\begin{array}{r} 15 \\ -\ 9 \\ \hline \end{array}$
22. $\begin{array}{r} 11 \\ -\ 2 \\ \hline \end{array}$
23. $\begin{array}{r} 16 \\ -\ 9 \\ \hline \end{array}$
24. $\begin{array}{r} 15 \\ -\ 7 \\ \hline \end{array}$

25. $\begin{array}{r} 13 \\ -\ 4 \\ \hline \end{array}$
26. $\begin{array}{r} 13 \\ -\ 8 \\ \hline \end{array}$
27. $\begin{array}{r} 10 \\ -\ 8 \\ \hline \end{array}$

Differences from 10 to 18

Solve each problem.

You're a Winner!

1. $18 - 9 =$ 2. $10 - 5 =$ 3. $13 - 7 =$

4. $14 - 6 =$ 5. $15 - 6 =$ 6. $12 - 3 =$

7. $15 - 7 =$ 8. $14 - 9 =$ 9. $17 - 8 =$

10. $11 - 7 =$ 11. $13 - 4 =$ 12. $11 - 4 =$

13. $12 - 6 =$ 14. $15 - 9 =$ 15. $11 - 5 =$

16. $10 - 1 =$ 17. $14 - 8 =$ 18. $16 - 8 =$

19. $10 - 2 =$ 20. $13 - 5 =$ 21. $10 - 8 =$

22. $11 - 2 =$ 23. $10 - 9 =$

24. $11 - 8 =$ 25. $13 - 8 =$

26. $17 - 9 =$ 27. $16 - 7 =$

Addition and Subtraction Through 6

Solve each problem.

Build Your Math Skills!

1. $\begin{array}{r} 4 \\ -0 \\ \hline \end{array}$ 2. $\begin{array}{r} 4 \\ +0 \\ \hline \end{array}$ 3. $\begin{array}{r} 0 \\ +3 \\ \hline \end{array}$ 4. $\begin{array}{r} 1 \\ +1 \\ \hline \end{array}$ 5. $\begin{array}{r} 2 \\ -1 \\ \hline \end{array}$ 6. $\begin{array}{r} 1 \\ +4 \\ \hline \end{array}$

7. $\begin{array}{r} 2 \\ +3 \\ \hline \end{array}$ 8. $\begin{array}{r} 3 \\ +2 \\ \hline \end{array}$ 9. $\begin{array}{r} 6 \\ -6 \\ \hline \end{array}$ 10. $\begin{array}{r} 4 \\ -3 \\ \hline \end{array}$ 11. $\begin{array}{r} 1 \\ +4 \\ \hline \end{array}$ 12. $\begin{array}{r} 1 \\ +3 \\ \hline \end{array}$

13. $\begin{array}{r} 5 \\ -2 \\ \hline \end{array}$ 14. $\begin{array}{r} 2 \\ -2 \\ \hline \end{array}$ 15. $\begin{array}{r} 4 \\ -2 \\ \hline \end{array}$ 16. $\begin{array}{r} 2 \\ +1 \\ \hline \end{array}$ 17. $\begin{array}{r} 2 \\ +2 \\ \hline \end{array}$ 18. $\begin{array}{r} 3 \\ -3 \\ \hline \end{array}$

19. $\begin{array}{r} 6 \\ -2 \\ \hline \end{array}$ 20. $\begin{array}{r} 6 \\ -5 \\ \hline \end{array}$ 21. $\begin{array}{r} 4 \\ +1 \\ \hline \end{array}$ 22. $\begin{array}{r} 2 \\ +3 \\ \hline \end{array}$ 23. $\begin{array}{r} 6 \\ -1 \\ \hline \end{array}$ 24. $\begin{array}{r} 3 \\ -1 \\ \hline \end{array}$

25. $\begin{array}{r} 5 \\ -1 \\ \hline \end{array}$ 26. $\begin{array}{r} 1 \\ +0 \\ \hline \end{array}$ 27. $\begin{array}{r} 6 \\ +0 \\ \hline \end{array}$

Addition and Subtraction Through 6

Total Problems: **27**
Problems Correct: _____

Solve each problem.

One Bite at a Time!

1. $\begin{array}{r} 6 \\ -0 \\ \hline \end{array}$
2. $\begin{array}{r} 1 \\ +0 \\ \hline \end{array}$
3. $\begin{array}{r} 2 \\ +3 \\ \hline \end{array}$
4. $\begin{array}{r} 4 \\ +1 \\ \hline \end{array}$
5. $\begin{array}{r} 5 \\ -1 \\ \hline \end{array}$
6. $\begin{array}{r} 4 \\ +1 \\ \hline \end{array}$

7. $\begin{array}{r} 4 \\ +0 \\ \hline \end{array}$
8. $\begin{array}{r} 3 \\ +2 \\ \hline \end{array}$
9. $\begin{array}{r} 6 \\ -6 \\ \hline \end{array}$
10. $\begin{array}{r} 3 \\ +3 \\ \hline \end{array}$
11. $\begin{array}{r} 2 \\ +1 \\ \hline \end{array}$
12. $\begin{array}{r} 1 \\ +3 \\ \hline \end{array}$

13. $\begin{array}{r} 4 \\ -2 \\ \hline \end{array}$
14. $\begin{array}{r} 5 \\ -2 \\ \hline \end{array}$
15. $\begin{array}{r} 2 \\ -2 \\ \hline \end{array}$
16. $\begin{array}{r} 4 \\ +1 \\ \hline \end{array}$
17. $\begin{array}{r} 2 \\ +2 \\ \hline \end{array}$
18. $\begin{array}{r} 4 \\ -3 \\ \hline \end{array}$

19. $\begin{array}{r} 6 \\ -2 \\ \hline \end{array}$
20. $\begin{array}{r} 6 \\ -5 \\ \hline \end{array}$
21. $\begin{array}{r} 1 \\ +1 \\ \hline \end{array}$
22. $\begin{array}{r} 2 \\ +3 \\ \hline \end{array}$
23. $\begin{array}{r} 3 \\ -1 \\ \hline \end{array}$
24. $\begin{array}{r} 2 \\ -1 \\ \hline \end{array}$

25. $\begin{array}{r} 6 \\ -1 \\ \hline \end{array}$
26. $\begin{array}{r} 6 \\ +0 \\ \hline \end{array}$
27. $\begin{array}{r} 0 \\ +3 \\ \hline \end{array}$

Addition and Subtraction Through 6

| Total Problems: | **27** |
| Problems Correct: | _____ |

Solve each problem.

Whale of a Job!

1. $3 + 3 =$

2. $5 - 1 =$

3. $2 + 2 =$

4. $4 - 2 =$

5. $4 + 2 =$

6. $2 - 1 =$

7. $0 + 5 =$

8. $3 - 2 =$

9. $7 - 2 =$

10. $3 + 1 =$

11. $2 - 1 =$

12. $1 + 3 =$

13. $0 - 0 =$

14. $1 + 2 =$

15. $6 - 5 =$

16. $2 + 4 =$

17. $6 - 2 =$

18. $7 - 1 =$

19. $0 + 6 =$

20. $6 - 2 =$

21. $1 + 5 =$

22. $6 - 3 =$

23. $1 + 4 =$

24. $5 - 4 =$

25. $3 + 2 =$

26. $4 - 1 =$

27. $6 + 0 =$

Addition and Subtraction Through 10

Total Problems:	27
Problems Correct:	_____

Solve each problem.

Look at You Go!

1. $\begin{array}{r} 10 \\ -\ 6 \\ \hline \end{array}$ 2. $\begin{array}{r} 9 \\ +\ 1 \\ \hline \end{array}$ 3. $\begin{array}{r} 6 \\ +\ 3 \\ \hline \end{array}$ 4. $\begin{array}{r} 8 \\ +\ 1 \\ \hline \end{array}$ 5. $\begin{array}{r} 9 \\ -\ 5 \\ \hline \end{array}$ 6. $\begin{array}{r} 6 \\ +\ 4 \\ \hline \end{array}$

7. $\begin{array}{r} 2 \\ +\ 3 \\ \hline \end{array}$ 8. $\begin{array}{r} 3 \\ +\ 5 \\ \hline \end{array}$ 9. $\begin{array}{r} 9 \\ -\ 0 \\ \hline \end{array}$ 10. $\begin{array}{r} 6 \\ -\ 2 \\ \hline \end{array}$ 11. $\begin{array}{r} 7 \\ +\ 1 \\ \hline \end{array}$ 12. $\begin{array}{r} 0 \\ +\ 3 \\ \hline \end{array}$

13. $\begin{array}{r} 8 \\ -\ 4 \\ \hline \end{array}$ 14. $\begin{array}{r} 5 \\ -\ 1 \\ \hline \end{array}$ 15. $\begin{array}{r} 10 \\ -\ 2 \\ \hline \end{array}$ 16. $\begin{array}{r} 4 \\ +\ 4 \\ \hline \end{array}$ 17. $\begin{array}{r} 8 \\ +\ 2 \\ \hline \end{array}$ 18. $\begin{array}{r} 9 \\ -\ 4 \\ \hline \end{array}$

19. $\begin{array}{r} 6 \\ -\ 3 \\ \hline \end{array}$ 20. $\begin{array}{r} 10 \\ -\ 5 \\ \hline \end{array}$ 21. $\begin{array}{r} 9 \\ +\ 0 \\ \hline \end{array}$ 22. $\begin{array}{r} 7 \\ +\ 3 \\ \hline \end{array}$ 23. $\begin{array}{r} 9 \\ -\ 6 \\ \hline \end{array}$ 24. $\begin{array}{r} 7 \\ -\ 7 \\ \hline \end{array}$

25. $\begin{array}{r} 8 \\ -\ 5 \\ \hline \end{array}$ 26. $\begin{array}{r} 5 \\ +\ 4 \\ \hline \end{array}$ 27. $\begin{array}{r} 6 \\ +\ 2 \\ \hline \end{array}$

Name _____ Date _____

Addition and Subtraction Through 10

Solve each problem.

Who-oo Likes to Add and Subtract?

1. 8
   − 5

2. 5
   + 5

3. 2
   + 7

4. 7
   + 3

5. 9
   − 6

6. 5
   + 4

7. 6
   + 3

8. 2
   + 6

9. 10
   − 4

10. 8
    + 2

11. 5
    + 1

12. 6
    − 3

13. 9
    − 4

14. 8
    − 7

15. 9
    + 1

16. 3
    + 4

17. 8
    − 2

18. 10
    − 10

19. 9
    − 3

20. 2
    + 3

21. 5
    + 3

22. 5
    − 4

23. 8
    − 4

24. 7
    − 4

25. 6
    + 4

26. 6
    + 2

27. 5
    + 3

Addition and Subtraction Through 10

Solve each problem.

Get Moving!

1. $6 + 3 =$ 2. $8 - 6 =$ 3. $5 + 3 =$

4. $10 - 0 =$ 5. $9 + 0 =$ 6. $9 - 1 =$

7. $8 + 1 =$ 8. $6 + 3 =$ 9. $7 - 2 =$

10. $5 + 1 =$ 11. $9 - 2 =$ 12. $5 + 4 =$

13. $6 - 4 =$ 14. $7 + 3 =$ 15. $8 - 2 =$

16. $2 + 6 =$ 17. $10 - 6 =$ 18. $10 - 1 =$

19. $6 + 4 =$ 20. $8 - 2 =$ 21. $2 + 7 =$

22. $8 - 5 =$ 23. $5 + 5 =$

24. $10 - 10 =$ 25. $3 + 4 =$

26. $9 - 3 =$ 27. $9 + 1 =$

Addition and Subtraction Through 10

Total Problems: **27**
Problems Correct: _____

Solve each problem.

Ready! Set! Add and Subtract!

1. $\begin{array}{r} 5 \\ -2 \\ \hline \end{array}$
2. $\begin{array}{r} 6 \\ +3 \\ \hline \end{array}$
3. $\begin{array}{r} 5 \\ +2 \\ \hline \end{array}$
4. $\begin{array}{r} 5 \\ +3 \\ \hline \end{array}$
5. $\begin{array}{r} 3 \\ -1 \\ \hline \end{array}$
6. $\begin{array}{r} 4 \\ +3 \\ \hline \end{array}$

7. $\begin{array}{r} 7 \\ +3 \\ \hline \end{array}$
8. $\begin{array}{r} 4 \\ +2 \\ \hline \end{array}$
9. $\begin{array}{r} 8 \\ -6 \\ \hline \end{array}$
10. $\begin{array}{r} 9 \\ -8 \\ \hline \end{array}$
11. $\begin{array}{r} 4 \\ +1 \\ \hline \end{array}$
12. $\begin{array}{r} 1 \\ +9 \\ \hline \end{array}$

13. $\begin{array}{r} 10 \\ -5 \\ \hline \end{array}$
14. $\begin{array}{r} 7 \\ -5 \\ \hline \end{array}$
15. $\begin{array}{r} 5 \\ -2 \\ \hline \end{array}$
16. $\begin{array}{r} 5 \\ +5 \\ \hline \end{array}$
17. $\begin{array}{r} 2 \\ +8 \\ \hline \end{array}$
18. $\begin{array}{r} 6 \\ -2 \\ \hline \end{array}$

19. $\begin{array}{r} 6 \\ -3 \\ \hline \end{array}$
20. $\begin{array}{r} 8 \\ -4 \\ \hline \end{array}$
21. $\begin{array}{r} 1 \\ +5 \\ \hline \end{array}$
22. $\begin{array}{r} 2 \\ +3 \\ \hline \end{array}$
23. $\begin{array}{r} 5 \\ -1 \\ \hline \end{array}$
24. $\begin{array}{r} 9 \\ -5 \\ \hline \end{array}$

25. $\begin{array}{r} 7 \\ -7 \\ \hline \end{array}$
26. $\begin{array}{r} 4 \\ +2 \\ \hline \end{array}$
27. $\begin{array}{r} 6 \\ +4 \\ \hline \end{array}$

Addition and Subtraction Through 11

Solve each problem.

Math Is Smooth Sailing!

1. $\begin{array}{r} 10 \\ -\ 7 \\ \hline \end{array}$

2. $\begin{array}{r} 7 \\ +\ 3 \\ \hline \end{array}$

3. $\begin{array}{r} 9 \\ +\ 1 \\ \hline \end{array}$

4. $\begin{array}{r} 6 \\ +\ 5 \\ \hline \end{array}$

5. $\begin{array}{r} 10 \\ -\ 3 \\ \hline \end{array}$

6. $\begin{array}{r} 6 \\ +\ 4 \\ \hline \end{array}$

7. $\begin{array}{r} 7 \\ +\ 3 \\ \hline \end{array}$

8. $\begin{array}{r} 5 \\ +\ 6 \\ \hline \end{array}$

9. $\begin{array}{r} 11 \\ -\ 4 \\ \hline \end{array}$

10. $\begin{array}{r} 11 \\ -\ 9 \\ \hline \end{array}$

11. $\begin{array}{r} 5 \\ +\ 4 \\ \hline \end{array}$

12. $\begin{array}{r} 4 \\ +\ 7 \\ \hline \end{array}$

13. $\begin{array}{r} 11 \\ -\ 2 \\ \hline \end{array}$

14. $\begin{array}{r} 10 \\ -\ 4 \\ \hline \end{array}$

15. $\begin{array}{r} 9 \\ -\ 2 \\ \hline \end{array}$

16. $\begin{array}{r} 7 \\ +\ 3 \\ \hline \end{array}$

17. $\begin{array}{r} 9 \\ +\ 2 \\ \hline \end{array}$

18. $\begin{array}{r} 10 \\ -\ 8 \\ \hline \end{array}$

19. $\begin{array}{r} 11 \\ -\ 7 \\ \hline \end{array}$

20. $\begin{array}{r} 10 \\ -\ 5 \\ \hline \end{array}$

21. $\begin{array}{r} 10 \\ +\ 1 \\ \hline \end{array}$

22. $\begin{array}{r} 8 \\ +\ 3 \\ \hline \end{array}$

23. $\begin{array}{r} 11 \\ -\ 6 \\ \hline \end{array}$

24. $\begin{array}{r} 10 \\ -\ 6 \\ \hline \end{array}$

25. $\begin{array}{r} 8 \\ -\ 1 \\ \hline \end{array}$

26. $\begin{array}{r} 8 \\ +\ 2 \\ \hline \end{array}$

27. $\begin{array}{r} 5 \\ +\ 5 \\ \hline \end{array}$

Name _____   Date _____

Addition and Subtraction Through 12

Solve each problem.

Mix It Up!

1. $\begin{array}{r} 10 \\ -\ 7 \\ \hline \end{array}$
2. $\begin{array}{r} 3 \\ +\ 8 \\ \hline \end{array}$
3. $\begin{array}{r} 6 \\ +\ 6 \\ \hline \end{array}$
4. $\begin{array}{r} 6 \\ +\ 3 \\ \hline \end{array}$
5. $\begin{array}{r} 11 \\ -\ 5 \\ \hline \end{array}$
6. $\begin{array}{r} 12 \\ -\ 2 \\ \hline \end{array}$

7. $\begin{array}{r} 6 \\ +\ 5 \\ \hline \end{array}$
8. $\begin{array}{r} 8 \\ +\ 4 \\ \hline \end{array}$
9. $\begin{array}{r} 10 \\ -\ 4 \\ \hline \end{array}$
10. $\begin{array}{r} 11 \\ -\ 3 \\ \hline \end{array}$
11. $\begin{array}{r} 9 \\ +\ 2 \\ \hline \end{array}$
12. $\begin{array}{r} 7 \\ +\ 3 \\ \hline \end{array}$

13. $\begin{array}{r} 11 \\ -\ 4 \\ \hline \end{array}$
14. $\begin{array}{r} 11 \\ -\ 2 \\ \hline \end{array}$
15. $\begin{array}{r} 12 \\ -\ 4 \\ \hline \end{array}$
16. $\begin{array}{r} 6 \\ +\ 5 \\ \hline \end{array}$
17. $\begin{array}{r} 5 \\ +\ 2 \\ \hline \end{array}$
18. $\begin{array}{r} 12 \\ -\ 5 \\ \hline \end{array}$

19. $\begin{array}{r} 12 \\ -\ 3 \\ \hline \end{array}$
20. $\begin{array}{r} 11 \\ -\ 6 \\ \hline \end{array}$
21. $\begin{array}{r} 8 \\ +\ 2 \\ \hline \end{array}$
22. $\begin{array}{r} 9 \\ +\ 3 \\ \hline \end{array}$
23. $\begin{array}{r} 11 \\ -\ 8 \\ \hline \end{array}$
24. $\begin{array}{r} 12 \\ -\ 6 \\ \hline \end{array}$

25. $\begin{array}{r} 10 \\ -\ 1 \\ \hline \end{array}$
26. $\begin{array}{r} 7 \\ +\ 5 \\ \hline \end{array}$
27. $\begin{array}{r} 5 \\ +\ 5 \\ \hline \end{array}$

Addition and Subtraction Through 14

Solve each problem.

Spread Your Math Wings!

1.	2.	3.	4.	5.	6.
12 $-\ 7$	9 $+\ 0$	5 $+\ 7$	8 $+\ 5$	14 $-\ 8$	6 $+\ 4$

7.	8.	9.	10.	11.	12.
5 $+\ 9$	6 $+\ 7$	11 $-\ 6$	13 $-\ 8$	6 $+\ 8$	7 $+\ 7$

13.	14.	15.	16.	17.	18.
12 $-\ 5$	10 $-\ 2$	11 $-\ 8$	8 $+\ 5$	2 $+\ 9$	12 $-\ 6$

19.	20.	21.	22.	23.	24.
12 $-\ 3$	13 $-\ 7$	5 $+\ 6$	3 $+\ 9$	13 $-\ 4$	10 $-\ 1$

25.	26.	27.
14 $-\ 7$	4 $+\ 8$	8 $+\ 4$

Name _____ Date _____

Addition and Subtraction Through 18

Solve each problem.

Relax with Math!

1. $15 - 6$

2. $9 + 9$

3. $6 + 9$

4. $12 + 1$

5. $12 - 9$

6. $8 + 9$

7. $6 + 7$

8. $10 + 2$

9. $13 - 6$

10. $15 - 7$

11. $8 + 8$

12. $8 + 3$

13. $16 - 8$

14. $15 - 8$

15. $11 - 2$

16. $9 + 2$

17. $14 + 2$

18. $18 - 9$

19. $14 - 6$

20. $15 - 5$

21. $4 + 9$

22. $7 + 8$

23. $16 - 7$

24. $17 - 9$

25. $15 - 9$

26. $11 + 5$

27. $16 + 0$

Name _____   Date _____

Missing Addends

Solve each problem.

Discover Missing Addends!

1. 6
   +☐
   ‾‾
    8

2. 0
   +☐
   ‾‾
    7

3. 1
   +☐
   ‾‾
    7

4. 4
   +☐
   ‾‾
    8

5. 8
   +☐
   ‾‾
    9

6. 1
   +☐
   ‾‾
    2

7. 2
   +☐
   ‾‾
    9

8. 3
   +☐
   ‾‾
   10

9. 2
   +☐
   ‾‾
    5

10. 4
    +☐
    ‾‾
     5

11. 4
    +☐
    ‾‾
    10

12. 6
    +☐
    ‾‾
     9

13. 1
    +☐
    ‾‾
     6

14. 3
    +☐
    ‾‾
     9

15. 8
    +☐
    ‾‾
    10

16. 7
    +☐
    ‾‾
     7

17. 2
    +☐
    ‾‾
     7

18. 5
    +☐
    ‾‾
     9

19. 6
    +☐
    ‾‾
    10

20. 6
    +☐
    ‾‾
     8

21. 2
    +☐
    ‾‾
    10

22. 3
    +☐
    ‾‾
     5

23. 3
    +☐
    ‾‾
     7

24. 4
    +☐
    ‾‾
     8

25. 2
    +☐
    ‾‾
     5

26. 5
    +☐
    ‾‾
     9

27. 7
    +☐
    ‾‾
     9

Name _____   Date _____

Missing Addends

Solve each problem.

Finding Missing Addends Is a Breeze!

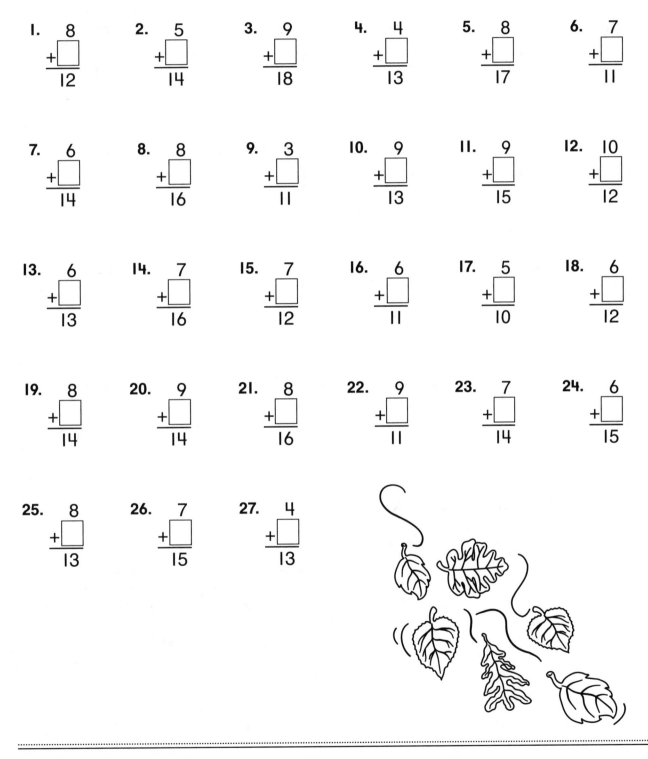

1. 8
   +☐
   ‾‾‾
   12

2. 5
   +☐
   ‾‾‾
   14

3. 9
   +☐
   ‾‾‾
   18

4. 4
   +☐
   ‾‾‾
   13

5. 8
   +☐
   ‾‾‾
   17

6. 7
   +☐
   ‾‾‾
   11

7. 6
   +☐
   ‾‾‾
   14

8. 8
   +☐
   ‾‾‾
   16

9. 3
   +☐
   ‾‾‾
   11

10. 9
    +☐
    ‾‾‾
    13

11. 9
    +☐
    ‾‾‾
    15

12. 10
    +☐
    ‾‾‾
    12

13. 6
    +☐
    ‾‾‾
    13

14. 7
    +☐
    ‾‾‾
    16

15. 7
    +☐
    ‾‾‾
    12

16. 6
    +☐
    ‾‾‾
    11

17. 5
    +☐
    ‾‾‾
    10

18. 6
    +☐
    ‾‾‾
    12

19. 8
    +☐
    ‾‾‾
    14

20. 9
    +☐
    ‾‾‾
    14

21. 8
    +☐
    ‾‾‾
    16

22. 9
    +☐
    ‾‾‾
    11

23. 7
    +☐
    ‾‾‾
    14

24. 6
    +☐
    ‾‾‾
    15

25. 8
    +☐
    ‾‾‾
    13

26. 7
    +☐
    ‾‾‾
    15

27. 4
    +☐
    ‾‾‾
    13

Name _____   Date _____

Missing Addends

Solve each problem.

Find the Missing Pieces!

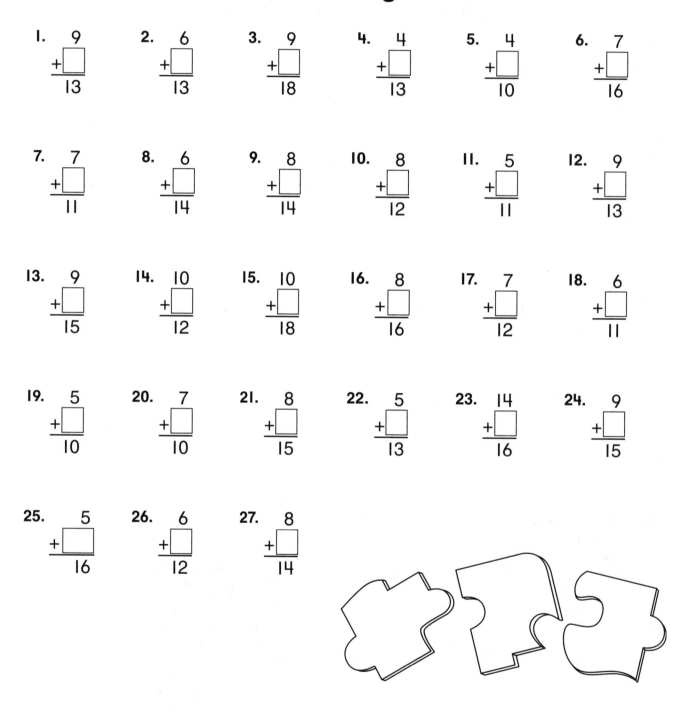

1. 9
   + ☐
   ‾‾‾
    13

2. 6
   + ☐
   ‾‾‾
    13

3. 9
   + ☐
   ‾‾‾
    18

4. 4
   + ☐
   ‾‾‾
    13

5. 4
   + ☐
   ‾‾‾
    10

6. 7
   + ☐
   ‾‾‾
    16

7. 7
   + ☐
   ‾‾‾
    11

8. 6
   + ☐
   ‾‾‾
    14

9. 8
   + ☐
   ‾‾‾
    14

10. 8
    + ☐
    ‾‾‾
     12

11. 5
    + ☐
    ‾‾‾
     11

12. 9
    + ☐
    ‾‾‾
     13

13. 9
    + ☐
    ‾‾‾
     15

14. 10
    + ☐
    ‾‾‾
     12

15. 10
    + ☐
    ‾‾‾
     18

16. 8
    + ☐
    ‾‾‾
     16

17. 7
    + ☐
    ‾‾‾
     12

18. 6
    + ☐
    ‾‾‾
     11

19. 5
    + ☐
    ‾‾‾
     10

20. 7
    + ☐
    ‾‾‾
     10

21. 8
    + ☐
    ‾‾‾
     15

22. 5
    + ☐
    ‾‾‾
     13

23. 14
    + ☐
    ‾‾‾
     16

24. 9
    + ☐
    ‾‾‾
     15

25. 5
    + ☐
    ‾‾‾
     16

26. 6
    + ☐
    ‾‾‾
     12

27. 8
    + ☐
    ‾‾‾
     14

Addition with Three Addends

Solve each problem.

Build Your Addition Skills!

1.   1
     1
  + 4

2.   5
     0
  + 1

3.   2
     2
  + 2

4.   1
     1
  + 1

5.   6
     0
  + 0

6.   3
     0
  + 2

7.   1
     2
  + 3

8.   2
     4
  + 0

9.   1
     2
  + 2

10.   4
      1
   + 0

11.   3
      0
   + 2

12.   3
      1
   + 1

13.   0
      3
   + 1

14.   3
      1
   + 1

15.   3
      0
   + 3

16.   2
      1
   + 1

17.   1
      0
   + 5

18.   5
      1
   + 0

19.   2
      4
   + 0

20.   4
      2
   + 0

21.   3
      0
   + 0

22.   2
      2
   + 1

23.   2
      2
   + 2

24.   1
      1
   + 3

25.   5
      0
   + 0

26.   2
      1
   + 3

27.   0
      0
   + 0

Addition with Three Addends

Solve each problem.

Addition Is a Breeze!

1. $3 + 1 + 1 =$

2. $4 + 1 + 1 =$

3. $1 + 0 + 1 =$

4. $1 + 2 + 2 =$

5. $4 + 6 + 7 =$

6. $2 + 2 + 2 =$

7. $4 + 6 + 3 =$

8. $1 + 2 + 3 =$

9. $4 + 0 + 2 =$

10. $1 + 1 + 2 =$

11. $0 + 4 + 1 =$

12. $0 + 2 + 4 =$

13. $4 + 2 + 0 =$

14. $3 + 1 + 0 =$

15. $0 + 2 + 3 =$

16. $2 + 1 + 0 =$

17. $2 + 1 + 1 =$

18. $3 + 0 + 1 =$

19. $2 + 0 + 2 =$

20. $1 + 2 + 1 =$

21. $2 + 0 + 1 =$

22. $3 + 0 + 2 =$

23. $3 + 1 + 2 =$

24. $1 + 1 + 3 =$

25. $1 + 1 + 1 =$

26. $0 + 3 + 1 =$

27. $2 + 0 + 3 =$

Addition with Three Addends

Solve each problem.

Think About It!

1. 5
    4
  + 1
  _____

2. 2
    3
  + 5
  _____

3. 2
    2
  + 4
  _____

4. 3
    3
  + 3
  _____

5. 2
    2
  + 5
  _____

6. 1
    3
  + 6
  _____

7. 1
    5
  + 2
  _____

8. 2
    2
  + 6
  _____

9. 1
    6
  + 2
  _____

10. 2
     0
   + 8
   _____

11. 2
     3
   + 3
   _____

12. 3
     7
   + 0
   _____

13. 7
     2
   + 1
   _____

14. 4
     1
   + 3
   _____

15. 5
     5
   + 0
   _____

16. 3
     4
   + 2
   _____

17. 2
     8
   + 0
   _____

18. 5
     1
   + 0
   _____

19. 7
     0
   + 2
   _____

20. 8
     1
   + 1
   _____

21. 3
     2
   + 3
   _____

22. 3
     4
   + 1
   _____

23. 3
     3
   + 3
   _____

24. 2
     0
   + 8
   _____

25. 3
     4
   + 3
   _____

26. 1
     8
   + 1
   _____

27. 5
     0
   + 4
   _____

Addition with Three Addends

Solve each problem.

Take a Close Look!

1. $2 + 0 + 3 =$

2. $5 + 3 + 1 =$

3. $6 + 2 + 0 =$

4. $6 + 3 + 1 =$

5. $6 + 0 + 1 =$

6. $4 + 0 + 2 =$

7. $3 + 0 + 4 =$

8. $3 + 3 + 3 =$

9. $2 + 2 + 6 =$

10. $7 + 0 + 1 =$

11. $2 + 3 + 2 =$

12. $8 + 0 + 1 =$

13. $5 + 1 + 1 =$

14. $3 + 6 + 1 =$

15. $2 + 2 + 2 =$

16. $7 + 2 + 1 =$

17. $5 + 2 + 3 =$

18. $6 + 1 + 0 =$

19. $2 + 4 + 1 =$

20. $5 + 1 + 3 =$

21. $4 + 2 + 3 =$

22. $3 + 0 + 3 =$

23. $3 + 3 + 2 =$

24. $6 + 2 + 0 =$

25. $6 + 1 + 2 =$

26. $5 + 4 + 1 =$

27. $6 + 3 + 1 =$

Addition with Three Addends

Solve each problem.

One Bite at a Time!

1. 9
    0
    + 4

2. 10
    0
    + 5

3. 2
    3
    + 6

4. 3
    4
    + 7

5. 2
    8
    + 5

6. 6
    0
    + 5

7. 12
    5
    + 6

8. 2
    9
    + 2

9. 4
    1
    + 9

10. 2
    3
    + 6

11. 8
    1
    + 7

12. 5
    2
    + 6

13. 11
    7
    + 1

14. 11
    7
    + 6

15. 6
    2
    + 4

16. 7
    0
    + 7

17. 4
    1
    + 6

18. 3
    9
    + 4

19. 1
    5
    + 6

20. 1
    7
    + 6

21. 5
    4
    + 7

22. 3
    2
    + 9

23. 12
    0
    + 6

24. 6
    6
    + 2

25. 3
    6
    + 9

26. 2
    4
    + 5

27. 9
    8
    + 0

Name _____ Date _____

Addition with Three Addends

Solve each problem.

Keep Up the Good Work!

| 1. | 5 3 +4 | 2. | 10 0 +5 | 3. | 7 2 +8 | 4. | 4 5 +2 | 5. | 2 3 +9 | 6. | 8 7 +2 |

1. 5
    3
  +4

2. 10
     0
  + 5

3. 7
    2
  +8

4. 4
    5
  +2

5. 2
    3
  +9

6. 8
    7
  +2

7. 4
    5
  +7

8. 6
    2
  +6

9. 3
    7
  +5

10. 4
     2
   +8

11. 1
     1
   +5

12. 4
     0
   +6

13. 2
     2
   +5

14. 3
     5
   +6

15. 5
     1
   +6

16. 11
      8
   + 8

17. 4
     8
   +4

18. 5
     7
   +4

19. 3
     9
   +3

20. 1
     3
   +8

21. 7
     1
   +5

22. 12
      0
   + 6

23. 5
     4
   +7

24. 3
     0
   +8

25. 4
     8
   +5

26. 9
     3
   +3

27. 10
      0
   +8

Name _____ Date _____

Two-Digit Addition

Solve each problem.

Jump to It!

1. 45
  + 30

2. 37
  + 22

3. 37
  + 30

4. 47
  + 31

5. 26
  + 53

6. 52
  + 42

7. 14
  + 34

8. 13
  + 43

9. 32
  + 51

10. 28
  + 51

11. 36
  + 41

12. 65
  + 34

13. 72
  + 12

14. 44
  + 25

15. 55
  + 22

16. 62
  + 34

17. 64
  + 25

18. 75
  + 24

19. 23
  + 14

20. 16
  + 60

21. 75
  + 24

22. 37
  + 51

23. 32
  + 47

24. 31
  + 48

25. 61
  + 26

26. 44
  + 32

27. 35
  + 44

Name _____ Date _____

Two-Digit Addition

Solve each problem.

Think Big!

1. 24
   + 24

2. 24
   + 23

3. 45
   + 30

4. 25
   + 61

5. 10
   + 50

6. 40
   + 40

7. 70
   + 18

8. 42
   + 17

9. 60
   + 20

10. 61
    + 27

11. 30
    + 40

12. 24
    + 44

13. 11
    + 75

14. 14
    + 24

15. 24
    + 35

16. 34
    + 12

17. 54
    + 13

18. 23
    + 44

19. 46
    + 53

20. 35
    + 13

21. 35
    + 34

22. 32
    + 26

23. 33
    + 42

24. 21
    + 52

25. 23
    + 52

26. 72
    + 14

27. 53
    + 23

Two-Digit Addition

Solve each problem.

A Smile Is Key!

1. $\begin{array}{r} 27 \\ + 82 \\ \hline \end{array}$
2. $\begin{array}{r} 74 \\ + 95 \\ \hline \end{array}$
3. $\begin{array}{r} 80 \\ + 60 \\ \hline \end{array}$
4. $\begin{array}{r} 95 \\ + 44 \\ \hline \end{array}$
5. $\begin{array}{r} 94 \\ + 93 \\ \hline \end{array}$
6. $\begin{array}{r} 41 \\ + 75 \\ \hline \end{array}$

7. $\begin{array}{r} 82 \\ + 71 \\ \hline \end{array}$
8. $\begin{array}{r} 97 \\ + 81 \\ \hline \end{array}$
9. $\begin{array}{r} 85 \\ + 91 \\ \hline \end{array}$
10. $\begin{array}{r} 33 \\ + 85 \\ \hline \end{array}$
11. $\begin{array}{r} 92 \\ + 54 \\ \hline \end{array}$
12. $\begin{array}{r} 74 \\ + 80 \\ \hline \end{array}$

13. $\begin{array}{r} 11 \\ + 75 \\ \hline \end{array}$
14. $\begin{array}{r} 53 \\ + 72 \\ \hline \end{array}$
15. $\begin{array}{r} 83 \\ + 84 \\ \hline \end{array}$
16. $\begin{array}{r} 52 \\ + 85 \\ \hline \end{array}$
17. $\begin{array}{r} 65 \\ + 42 \\ \hline \end{array}$
18. $\begin{array}{r} 94 \\ + 64 \\ \hline \end{array}$

19. $\begin{array}{r} 72 \\ + 72 \\ \hline \end{array}$
20. $\begin{array}{r} 95 \\ + 33 \\ \hline \end{array}$
21. $\begin{array}{r} 44 \\ + 92 \\ \hline \end{array}$
22. $\begin{array}{r} 52 \\ + 56 \\ \hline \end{array}$
23. $\begin{array}{r} 71 \\ + 66 \\ \hline \end{array}$
24. $\begin{array}{r} 60 \\ + 85 \\ \hline \end{array}$

25. $\begin{array}{r} 93 \\ + 26 \\ \hline \end{array}$
26. $\begin{array}{r} 32 \\ + 72 \\ \hline \end{array}$
27. $\begin{array}{r} 44 \\ + 84 \\ \hline \end{array}$

Two-Digit Addition

Solve each problem.

Math Is a Gift!

1. 16
   + 42

2. 51
   + 25

3. 37
   + 32

4. 76
   + 23

5. 11
   + 62

6. 12
   + 12

7. 31
   + 13

8. 38
   + 11

9. 12
   + 15

10. 43
   + 25

11. 34
   + 32

12. 55
   + 14

13. 15
   + 10

14. 35
   + 42

15. 23
   + 62

16. 70
   + 10

17. 57
   + 32

18. 45
   + 23

19. 20
   + 71

20. 56
   + 20

21. 21
   + 16

22. 42
   + 20

23. 65
   + 32

24. 32
   + 27

25. 24
   + 15

26. 54
   + 13

27. 52
   + 33

  CD-104318 • © Carson-Dellosa

Two-Digit Addition

Solve each problem.

Fly High with Addition!

1. 81
  + 10

2. 10
  + 60

3. 35
  + 43

4. 63
  + 21

5. 44
  + 23

6. 72
  + 17

7. 61
  + 26

8. 44
  + 34

9. 33
  + 42

10. 19
  + 20

11. 37
  + 22

12. 56
  + 32

13. 11
  + 75

14. 62
  + 36

15. 25
  + 32

16. 12
  + 21

17. 21
  + 25

18. 14
  + 41

19. 23
  + 53

20. 42
  + 21

21. 60
  + 34

22. 12
  + 46

23. 28
  + 61

24. 11
  + 18

25. 45
  + 14

26. 41
  + 41

27. 15
  + 11

Two-Digit Addition with Regrouping

Solve each problem. Regroup when necessary.

Nice Work!

1. $\begin{array}{r} 17 \\ + 37 \\ \hline \end{array}$

2. $\begin{array}{r} 23 \\ + 14 \\ \hline \end{array}$

3. $\begin{array}{r} 28 \\ + 24 \\ \hline \end{array}$

4. $\begin{array}{r} 47 \\ + 35 \\ \hline \end{array}$

5. $\begin{array}{r} 49 \\ + 11 \\ \hline \end{array}$

6. $\begin{array}{r} 36 \\ + 17 \\ \hline \end{array}$

7. $\begin{array}{r} 55 \\ + 33 \\ \hline \end{array}$

8. $\begin{array}{r} 12 \\ + 58 \\ \hline \end{array}$

9. $\begin{array}{r} 39 \\ + 39 \\ \hline \end{array}$

10. $\begin{array}{r} 48 \\ + 12 \\ \hline \end{array}$

11. $\begin{array}{r} 21 \\ + 22 \\ \hline \end{array}$

12. $\begin{array}{r} 77 \\ + 15 \\ \hline \end{array}$

13. $\begin{array}{r} 11 \\ + 75 \\ \hline \end{array}$

14. $\begin{array}{r} 16 \\ + 15 \\ \hline \end{array}$

15. $\begin{array}{r} 49 \\ + 24 \\ \hline \end{array}$

16. $\begin{array}{r} 29 \\ + 28 \\ \hline \end{array}$

17. $\begin{array}{r} 36 \\ + 54 \\ \hline \end{array}$

18. $\begin{array}{r} 32 \\ + 47 \\ \hline \end{array}$

19. $\begin{array}{r} 72 \\ + 22 \\ \hline \end{array}$

20. $\begin{array}{r} 57 \\ + 39 \\ \hline \end{array}$

21. $\begin{array}{r} 24 \\ + 44 \\ \hline \end{array}$

22. $\begin{array}{r} 67 \\ + 34 \\ \hline \end{array}$

23. $\begin{array}{r} 20 \\ + 16 \\ \hline \end{array}$

24. $\begin{array}{r} 56 \\ + 19 \\ \hline \end{array}$

25. $\begin{array}{r} 19 \\ + 67 \\ \hline \end{array}$

26. $\begin{array}{r} 68 \\ + 25 \\ \hline \end{array}$

27. $\begin{array}{r} 52 \\ + 43 \\ \hline \end{array}$

Name _____   Date _____

Two-Digit Addition with Regrouping

Solve each problem. Regroup when necessary.

Way to Step Up!

1. 49
  + 28

2. 18
  + 19

3. 29
  + 29

4. 66
  + 15

5. 18
  + 56

6. 38
  + 47

7. 47
  + 15

8. 58
  + 14

9. 57
  + 39

10. 66
   + 29

11. 67
   + 27

12. 38
   + 13

13. 28
   + 52

14. 27
   + 36

15. 28
   + 15

16. 39
   + 17

17. 35
   + 29

18. 26
   + 26

19. 34
   + 36

20. 38
   + 12

21. 23
   + 27

22. 34
   + 46

23. 17
   + 24

24. 19
   + 74

25. 16
   + 45

26. 49
   + 38

27. 59
   + 19

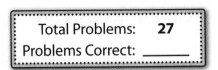

Name _____ Date _____

Two-Digit Addition with Regrouping

Total Problems: 27
Problems Correct: _____

Solve each problem. Regroup when necessary.

Math Is a Treasure!

1. 13
  + 28

2. 66
  + 27

3. 67
  + 18

4. 39
  + 14

5. 26
  + 59

6. 22
  + 18

7. 65
  + 26

8. 45
  + 19

9. 55
  + 37

10. 16
  + 16

11. 39
  + 38

12. 52
  + 28

13. 44
  + 39

14. 42
  + 29

15. 15
  + 28

16. 29
  + 23

17. 14
  + 49

18. 48
  + 27

19. 37
  + 17

20. 27
  + 19

21. 21
  + 39

22. 32
  + 39

23. 22
  + 28

24. 78
  + 19

25. 38
  + 36

26. 18
  + 18

27. 24
  + 56

CD-104318 • © Carson-Dellosa

Two-Digit Addition with Regrouping

Solve each problem. Regroup when necessary.

Munch on These Numbers!

1. 16
  + 45

2. 23
  + 27

3. 39
  + 17

4. 67
  + 27

5. 38
  + 13

6. 29
  + 29

7. 19
  + 74

8. 27
  + 36

9. 57
  + 37

10. 18
  + 16

11. 49
  + 52

12. 66
  + 77

13. 32
  + 99

14. 81
  + 89

15. 15
  + 44

16. 65
  + 78

17. 15
  + 29

18. 74
  + 55

19. 21
  + 63

20. 46
  + 98

21. 55
  + 39

22. 45
  + 37

23. 31
  + 56

24. 79
  + 59

25. 28
  + 19

26. 17
  + 13

27. 56
  + 56

Name _____   Date _____

Two-Digit Subtraction

Solve each problem.

Keep Rolling Along!

1. 63
− 40

2. 80
− 50

3. 75
− 52

4. 79
− 22

5. 38
− 15

6. 93
− 33

7. 67
− 46

8. 83
− 42

9. 77
− 11

10. 76
− 51

11. 59
− 37

12. 77
− 64

13. 56
− 36

14. 63
− 31

15. 48
− 26

16. 86
− 55

17. 40
− 20

18. 43
− 40

19. 87
− 35

20. 84
− 51

21. 15
− 10

22. 31
− 10

23. 77
− 34

24. 42
− 10

25. 64
− 30

26. 39
− 25

27. 87
− 12

Two-Digit Subtraction

Solve each problem.

Use Your Subtraction Tools!

1. $\begin{array}{r} 61 \\ -41 \\ \hline \end{array}$
2. $\begin{array}{r} 39 \\ -26 \\ \hline \end{array}$
3. $\begin{array}{r} 85 \\ -43 \\ \hline \end{array}$
4. $\begin{array}{r} 56 \\ -31 \\ \hline \end{array}$
5. $\begin{array}{r} 47 \\ -17 \\ \hline \end{array}$
6. $\begin{array}{r} 87 \\ -45 \\ \hline \end{array}$

7. $\begin{array}{r} 67 \\ -52 \\ \hline \end{array}$
8. $\begin{array}{r} 78 \\ -33 \\ \hline \end{array}$
9. $\begin{array}{r} 69 \\ -46 \\ \hline \end{array}$
10. $\begin{array}{r} 96 \\ -21 \\ \hline \end{array}$
11. $\begin{array}{r} 94 \\ -71 \\ \hline \end{array}$
12. $\begin{array}{r} 40 \\ -20 \\ \hline \end{array}$

13. $\begin{array}{r} 70 \\ -20 \\ \hline \end{array}$
14. $\begin{array}{r} 98 \\ -31 \\ \hline \end{array}$
15. $\begin{array}{r} 58 \\ -18 \\ \hline \end{array}$
16. $\begin{array}{r} 38 \\ -15 \\ \hline \end{array}$
17. $\begin{array}{r} 65 \\ -12 \\ \hline \end{array}$
18. $\begin{array}{r} 88 \\ -62 \\ \hline \end{array}$

19. $\begin{array}{r} 26 \\ -24 \\ \hline \end{array}$
20. $\begin{array}{r} 70 \\ -20 \\ \hline \end{array}$
21. $\begin{array}{r} 82 \\ -51 \\ \hline \end{array}$
22. $\begin{array}{r} 62 \\ -20 \\ \hline \end{array}$
23. $\begin{array}{r} 98 \\ -34 \\ \hline \end{array}$
24. $\begin{array}{r} 88 \\ -12 \\ \hline \end{array}$

25. $\begin{array}{r} 45 \\ -35 \\ \hline \end{array}$
26. $\begin{array}{r} 67 \\ -45 \\ \hline \end{array}$
27. $\begin{array}{r} 19 \\ -15 \\ \hline \end{array}$

Name _____ Date _____

Two-Digit Subtraction

Solve each problem.

Double the Fun!

1. 77
  − 44

2. 55
  − 22

3. 98
  − 53

4. 29
  − 14

5. 60
  − 50

6. 69
  − 22

7. 45
  − 25

8. 78
  − 61

9. 86
  − 82

10. 39
  − 13

11. 86
  − 24

12. 59
  − 51

13. 72
  − 31

14. 93
  − 81

15. 26
  − 11

16. 98
  − 14

17. 67
  − 32

18. 39
  − 13

19. 77
  − 10

20. 87
  − 15

21. 63
  − 30

22. 82
  − 71

23. 74
  − 53

24. 83
  − 42

25. 48
  − 26

26. 82
  − 22

27. 88
  − 24

Two-Digit Subtraction

Solve each problem.

Now You're Soaring!

1. 56
    $- 21$

2. 87
    $- 45$

3. 68
    $- 36$

4. 45
    $- 23$

5. 87
    $- 34$

6. 99
    $- 66$

7. 76
    $- 75$

8. 48
    $- 22$

9. 29
    $- 12$

10. 33
    $- 11$

11. 67
    $- 34$

12. 28
    $- 17$

13. 65
    $- 32$

14. 95
    $- 14$

15. 82
    $- 22$

16. 27
    $- 16$

17. 69
    $- 34$

18. 59
    $- 41$

19. 74
    $- 22$

20. 78
    $- 45$

21. 89
    $- 88$

22. 68
    $- 46$

23. 39
    $- 22$

24. 61
    $- 40$

25. 56
    $- 23$

26. 36
    $- 25$

27. 77
    $- 66$

Name _____ Date _____

Two-Digit Subtraction with Regrouping

Total Problems: **27**
Problems Correct: _____

Solve each problem. Regroup when necessary.

Take Your Time!

1. $\begin{array}{r} 61 \\ -29 \\ \hline \end{array}$
2. $\begin{array}{r} 91 \\ -49 \\ \hline \end{array}$
3. $\begin{array}{r} 66 \\ -18 \\ \hline \end{array}$
4. $\begin{array}{r} 78 \\ -54 \\ \hline \end{array}$
5. $\begin{array}{r} 31 \\ -15 \\ \hline \end{array}$
6. $\begin{array}{r} 73 \\ -57 \\ \hline \end{array}$

7. $\begin{array}{r} 40 \\ -23 \\ \hline \end{array}$
8. $\begin{array}{r} 51 \\ -42 \\ \hline \end{array}$
9. $\begin{array}{r} 77 \\ -23 \\ \hline \end{array}$
10. $\begin{array}{r} 87 \\ -58 \\ \hline \end{array}$
11. $\begin{array}{r} 96 \\ -45 \\ \hline \end{array}$
12. $\begin{array}{r} 34 \\ -27 \\ \hline \end{array}$

13. $\begin{array}{r} 85 \\ -36 \\ \hline \end{array}$
14. $\begin{array}{r} 50 \\ -25 \\ \hline \end{array}$
15. $\begin{array}{r} 26 \\ -11 \\ \hline \end{array}$
16. $\begin{array}{r} 63 \\ -24 \\ \hline \end{array}$
17. $\begin{array}{r} 86 \\ -69 \\ \hline \end{array}$
18. $\begin{array}{r} 98 \\ -39 \\ \hline \end{array}$

19. $\begin{array}{r} 97 \\ -48 \\ \hline \end{array}$
20. $\begin{array}{r} 96 \\ -32 \\ \hline \end{array}$
21. $\begin{array}{r} 79 \\ -56 \\ \hline \end{array}$
22. $\begin{array}{r} 53 \\ -28 \\ \hline \end{array}$
23. $\begin{array}{r} 24 \\ -17 \\ \hline \end{array}$
24. $\begin{array}{r} 52 \\ -44 \\ \hline \end{array}$

25. $\begin{array}{r} 43 \\ -18 \\ \hline \end{array}$
26. $\begin{array}{r} 54 \\ -32 \\ \hline \end{array}$
27. $\begin{array}{r} 41 \\ -28 \\ \hline \end{array}$

Name _____ Date _____

Two-Digit Subtraction with Regrouping

Solve each problem. Regroup when necessary.

Take It Slow and Easy!

1. 26
  − 18

2. 54
  − 46

3. 42
  − 33

4. 28
  − 19

5. 53
  − 46

6. 91
  − 24

7. 65
  − 46

8. 57
  − 48

9. 81
  − 72

10. 73
  − 64

11. 26
  − 18

12. 62
  − 49

13. 60
  − 37

14. 67
  − 49

15. 52
  − 43

16. 42
  − 33

17. 55
  − 47

18. 33
  − 26

19. 34
  − 27

20. 77
  − 68

21. 67
  − 19

22. 67
  − 59

23. 82
  − 45

24. 82
  − 73

25. 31
  − 19

26. 56
  − 47

27. 48
  − 39

Two-Digit Subtraction with Regrouping

Solve each problem. Regroup when necessary.

One Step at a Time!

1. 26
   − 19

2. 37
   − 18

3. 98
   − 49

4. 94
   − 25

5. 66
   − 48

6. 76
   − 28

7. 34
   − 17

8. 52
   − 23

9. 31
   − 27

10. 80
    − 38

11. 86
    − 47

12. 37
    − 28

13. 63
    − 26

14. 80
    − 12

15. 97
    − 69

16. 93
    − 28

17. 83
    − 57

18. 71
    − 16

19. 40
    − 38

20. 71
    − 33

21. 55
    − 27

22. 94
    − 35

23. 78
    − 49

24. 80
    − 35

25. 43
    − 38

26. 82
    − 37

27. 81
    − 24

Two-Digit Subtraction with Regrouping

Total Problems:	27
Problems Correct:	_____

Solve each problem. Regroup when necessary.

Practice, Practice, Practice!

1. 40 − 19	2. 75 − 23	3. 62 − 48	4. 79 − 73	5. 66 − 29	6. 90 − 11
7. 91 − 35	8. 56 − 27	9. 91 − 42	10. 98 − 41	11. 41 − 20	12. 94 − 86
13. 86 − 21	14. 28 − 18	15. 64 − 58	16. 84 − 25	17. 60 − 20	18. 49 − 37
19. 94 − 66	20. 68 − 33	21. 61 − 37	22. 52 − 33	23. 97 − 49	24. 46 − 12
25. 29 − 17	26. 63 − 40	27. 78 − 35			

Name _____   Date _____

Two-Digit Subtraction with Regrouping

Solve each problem. Regroup when necessary.

You're Out of This World!

1.　73
　 − 22

2.　80
　 − 14

3.　66
　 − 28

4.　46
　 − 35

5.　26
　 − 18

6.　87
　 − 38

7.　63
　 − 36

8.　52
　 − 28

9.　97
　 − 63

10.　34
　 − 27

11.　77
　 − 57

12.　34
　 − 29

13.　71
　 − 35

14.　35
　 − 26

15.　99
　 − 12

16.　53
　 − 44

17.　90
　 − 33

18.　93
　 − 15

19.　90
　 − 12

20.　82
　 − 39

21.　83
　 − 39

22.　43
　 − 12

23.　72
　 − 43

24.　57
　 − 48

25.　82
　 − 49

26.　78
　 − 65

27.　66
　 − 55

Two-Digit Addition and Subtraction

Solve each problem.

Going Up and Down!

1. $\begin{array}{r} 74 \\ -\ 30 \\ \hline \end{array}$	2. $\begin{array}{r} 76 \\ +\ 22 \\ \hline \end{array}$	3. $\begin{array}{r} 72 \\ +\ 23 \\ \hline \end{array}$	4. $\begin{array}{r} 74 \\ +\ 12 \\ \hline \end{array}$	5. $\begin{array}{r} 85 \\ -\ 61 \\ \hline \end{array}$	6. $\begin{array}{r} 45 \\ +\ 24 \\ \hline \end{array}$
7. $\begin{array}{r} 60 \\ +\ 34 \\ \hline \end{array}$	8. $\begin{array}{r} 78 \\ +\ 21 \\ \hline \end{array}$	9. $\begin{array}{r} 76 \\ -\ 26 \\ \hline \end{array}$	10. $\begin{array}{r} 43 \\ -\ 23 \\ \hline \end{array}$	11. $\begin{array}{r} 78 \\ -\ 21 \\ \hline \end{array}$	12. $\begin{array}{r} 43 \\ +\ 53 \\ \hline \end{array}$
13. $\begin{array}{r} 16 \\ +\ 12 \\ \hline \end{array}$	14. $\begin{array}{r} 54 \\ -\ 32 \\ \hline \end{array}$	15. $\begin{array}{r} 82 \\ -\ 42 \\ \hline \end{array}$	16. $\begin{array}{r} 33 \\ +\ 33 \\ \hline \end{array}$	17. $\begin{array}{r} 75 \\ +\ 24 \\ \hline \end{array}$	18. $\begin{array}{r} 64 \\ -\ 23 \\ \hline \end{array}$
19. $\begin{array}{r} 45 \\ -\ 21 \\ \hline \end{array}$	20. $\begin{array}{r} 76 \\ -\ 25 \\ \hline \end{array}$	21. $\begin{array}{r} 54 \\ +\ 45 \\ \hline \end{array}$	22. $\begin{array}{r} 67 \\ +\ 22 \\ \hline \end{array}$	23. $\begin{array}{r} 66 \\ -\ 51 \\ \hline \end{array}$	24. $\begin{array}{r} 83 \\ -\ 62 \\ \hline \end{array}$
25. $\begin{array}{r} 52 \\ -\ 31 \\ \hline \end{array}$	26. $\begin{array}{r} 34 \\ +\ 22 \\ \hline \end{array}$	27. $\begin{array}{r} 43 \\ +\ 34 \\ \hline \end{array}$			

Two-Digit Addition and Subtraction

Total Problems: **27**
Problems Correct: _____

Solve each problem.

Stepping Up to the Plate!

1. 77
   − 63

2. 17
   + 40

3. 44
   + 22

4. 76
   + 23

5. 86
   − 44

6. 42
   + 34

7. 27
   + 31

8. 55
   + 42

9. 77
   − 36

10. 47
    − 26

11. 24
    + 34

12. 78
    + 21

13. 95
    − 30

14. 95
    − 50

15. 75
    − 30

16. 72
    + 21

17. 62
    + 36

18. 57
    − 16

19. 57
    − 57

20. 36
    − 15

21. 61
    + 33

22. 43
    + 23

23. 83
    − 20

24. 89
    − 61

25. 69
    − 51

26. 38
    + 40

27. 75
    + 21

Name _____   Date _____

Two-Digit Addition and Subtraction with Regrouping

Solve each problem. Regroup when necessary.

Let's Get Rolling!

1. $\begin{array}{r} 32 \\ -16 \\ \hline \end{array}$ 2. $\begin{array}{r} 41 \\ +49 \\ \hline \end{array}$ 3. $\begin{array}{r} 67 \\ +28 \\ \hline \end{array}$ 4. $\begin{array}{r} 37 \\ +37 \\ \hline \end{array}$ 5. $\begin{array}{r} 59 \\ -44 \\ \hline \end{array}$ 6. $\begin{array}{r} 45 \\ +56 \\ \hline \end{array}$

7. $\begin{array}{r} 40 \\ +63 \\ \hline \end{array}$ 8. $\begin{array}{r} 78 \\ +46 \\ \hline \end{array}$ 9. $\begin{array}{r} 70 \\ -10 \\ \hline \end{array}$ 10. $\begin{array}{r} 73 \\ -63 \\ \hline \end{array}$ 11. $\begin{array}{r} 64 \\ +71 \\ \hline \end{array}$ 12. $\begin{array}{r} 90 \\ +34 \\ \hline \end{array}$

13. $\begin{array}{r} 66 \\ -30 \\ \hline \end{array}$ 14. $\begin{array}{r} 67 \\ -49 \\ \hline \end{array}$ 15. $\begin{array}{r} 92 \\ -57 \\ \hline \end{array}$ 16. $\begin{array}{r} 45 \\ +89 \\ \hline \end{array}$ 17. $\begin{array}{r} 32 \\ +32 \\ \hline \end{array}$ 18. $\begin{array}{r} 88 \\ -64 \\ \hline \end{array}$

19. $\begin{array}{r} 95 \\ -52 \\ \hline \end{array}$ 20. $\begin{array}{r} 79 \\ -26 \\ \hline \end{array}$ 21. $\begin{array}{r} 23 \\ +41 \\ \hline \end{array}$ 22. $\begin{array}{r} 82 \\ +53 \\ \hline \end{array}$ 23. $\begin{array}{r} 90 \\ -25 \\ \hline \end{array}$ 24. $\begin{array}{r} 73 \\ -41 \\ \hline \end{array}$

25. $\begin{array}{r} 98 \\ -21 \\ \hline \end{array}$ 26. $\begin{array}{r} 31 \\ +29 \\ \hline \end{array}$ 27. $\begin{array}{r} 76 \\ +47 \\ \hline \end{array}$

Name _____ Date _____

Two- and Three-Digit Addition

Solve each problem.

Addition Is a Walk in the Park!

1. 12 + 45

2. 44 + 35

3. 43 + 21

4. 70 + 29

5. 43 + 26

6. 440 + 150

7. 982 + 12

8. 323 + 433

9. 609 + 290

10. 44 + 22

11. 137 + 122

12. 251 + 540

13. 200 + 400

14. 521 + 342

15. 601 + 216

16. 175 + 22

17. 113 + 305

18. 181 + 14

19. 342 + 50

20. 576 + 103

21. 700 + 43

22. 645 + 223

23. 73 + 23

24. 121 + 131

25. 70 + 20

26. 443 + 53

27. 835 + 124

Three-Digit Addition

Solve each problem.

Go for It!

1. 486
    $+ 313$

2. 639
    $+ 250$

3. 387
    $+ 412$

4. 563
    $+ 416$

5. 574
    $+ 225$

6. 362
    $+ 332$

7. 667
    $+ 300$

8. 450
    $+ 246$

9. 738
    $+ 261$

10. 113
    $+ 215$

11. 532
    $+ 213$

12. 561
    $+ 238$

13. 342
    $+ 237$

14. 674
    $+ 225$

15. 437
    $+ 152$

16. 768
    $+ 221$

17. 342
    $+ 321$

18. 785
    $+ 113$

19. 834
    $+ 165$

20. 652
    $+ 234$

21. 460
    $+ 339$

22. 437
    $+ 232$

23. 434
    $+ 432$

24. 674
    $+ 225$

25. 856
    $+ 143$

26. 656
    $+ 223$

27. 435
    $+ 264$

Name _____   Date _____

Two- and Three-Digit Subtraction

Total Problems: **27**
Problems Correct: _____

Solve each problem.

Take a Shot!

1. 65
  − 33

2. 99
  − 45

3. 89
  − 56

4. 86
  − 23

5. 379
  − 163

6. 977
  − 431

7. 795
  − 461

8. 785
  − 243

9. 196
  − 81

10. 899
  − 276

11. 439
  − 121

12. 769
  − 342

13. 98
  − 46

14. 998
  − 354

15. 143
  − 33

16. 978
  − 453

17. 398
  − 346

18. 300
  − 200

19. 925
  − 14

20. 170
  − 130

21. 286
  − 166

22. 487
  − 267

23. 364
  − 50

24. 856
  − 113

25. 886
  − 332

26. 934
  − 211

27. 378
  − 245

CD-104318 • © Carson-Dellosa

Name _____ Date _____

Three-Digit Subtraction

Solve each problem.

Yes, You Can!

1. 887
   − 354

2. 427
   − 211

3. 674
   − 124

4. 675
   − 243

5. 697
   − 463

6. 715
   − 704

7. 400
   − 300

8. 856
   − 431

9. 498
   − 268

10. 397
   − 231

11. 333
   − 222

12. 745
   − 312

13. 786
   − 231

14. 869
   − 341

15. 847
   − 243

16. 879
   − 239

17. 632
   − 131

18. 678
   − 132

19. 849
   − 832

20. 770
   − 340

21. 657
   − 121

22. 387
   − 132

23. 879
   − 436

24. 418
   − 317

25. 680
   − 220

26. 834
   − 212

27. 356
   − 254

Three-Digit Addition and Subtraction with Regrouping

Solve each problem. Regroup when necessary.

Hang in There!

1. 539
   − 375

2. 476
   + 243

3. 176
   + 484

4. 392
   + 292

5. 787
   − 598

6. 165
   + 427

7. 481
   + 428

8. 842
   + 177

9. 762
   − 395

10. 856
   − 399

11. 347
   + 983

12. 275
   + 298

13. 628
   − 137

14. 531
   − 467

15. 496
   − 288

16. 389
   + 392

17. 276
   + 391

18. 374
   − 276

19. 983
   − 468

20. 834
   − 376

21. 452
   + 287

22. 392
   + 284

23. 597
   − 388

24. 584
   − 287

25. 498
   − 269

26. 735
   + 373

27. 392
   + 161

Name _____   Date _____

Multiplication with Factors 0 to 5

Solve each problem.

Leaping into Multiplication!

1. 5
  × 3

2. 3
  × 4

3. 5
  × 1

4. 2
  × 3

5. 1
  × 0

6. 5
  × 5

7. 1
  × 3

8. 2
  × 0

9. 2
  × 4

10. 2
  × 3

11. 2
  × 2

12. 4
  × 5

13. 3
  × 3

14. 4
  × 3

15. 4
  × 1

16. 3
  × 0

17. 5
  × 3

18. 2
  × 0

19. 2
  × 1

20. 1
  × 5

21. 1
  × 2

22. 1
  × 0

23. 4
  × 5

24. 1
  × 4

25. 3
  × 5

26. 5
  × 2

27. 5
  × 5

Multiplication with Factors 0 to 5

Total Problems:	27
Problems Correct:	_____

Solve each problem.

You Can Rock Multiplication!

1. $4 \times 5 =$ 2. $0 \times 0 =$ 3. $0 \times 5 =$

4. $5 \times 5 =$ 5. $2 \times 1 =$ 6. $3 \times 5 =$

7. $3 \times 2 =$ 8. $3 \times 1 =$ 9. $5 \times 2 =$

10. $2 \times 2 =$ 11. $2 \times 5 =$ 12. $4 \times 4 =$

13. $2 \times 3 =$ 14. $4 \times 1 =$ 15. $4 \times 3 =$

16. $0 \times 1 =$ 17. $4 \times 4 =$ 18. $0 \times 2 =$

19. $1 \times 3 =$ 20. $0 \times 4 =$ 21. $3 \times 3 =$

22. $1 \times 2 =$ 23. $5 \times 3 =$

24. $3 \times 4 =$ 25. $1 \times 1 =$

26. $2 \times 4 =$ 27. $5 \times 1 =$

CD-104318 • © Carson-Dellosa

Multiplication with Factors 0 to 5

Solve each problem.

Swinging Along!

1. $0 \times 2 =$ 2. $3 \times 3 =$ 3. $0 \times 5 =$

4. $5 \times 5 =$ 5. $4 \times 1 =$ 6. $3 \times 5 =$

7. $2 \times 2 =$ 8. $2 \times 5 =$ 9. $0 \times 4 =$

10. $5 \times 2 =$ 11. $3 \times 1 =$ 12. $4 \times 4 =$

13. $2 \times 3 =$ 14. $1 \times 5 =$ 15. $0 \times 1 =$

16. $4 \times 2 =$ 17. $5 \times 1 =$ 18. $4 \times 5 =$

19. $2 \times 2 =$ 20. $1 \times 3 =$ 21. $0 \times 0 =$

22. $1 \times 2 =$ 23. $5 \times 3 =$

24. $2 \times 1 =$ 25. $1 \times 1 =$

26. $4 \times 3 =$ 27. $5 \times 1 =$

Name _____ Date _____

Multiplication with Factors 0 to 5

Solve each problem.

You Did It!

1. $\begin{array}{r} 1 \\ \times 2 \\ \hline \end{array}$
2. $\begin{array}{r} 1 \\ \times 1 \\ \hline \end{array}$
3. $\begin{array}{r} 0 \\ \times 3 \\ \hline \end{array}$
4. $\begin{array}{r} 1 \\ \times 3 \\ \hline \end{array}$
5. $\begin{array}{r} 2 \\ \times 5 \\ \hline \end{array}$
6. $\begin{array}{r} 5 \\ \times 5 \\ \hline \end{array}$

7. $\begin{array}{r} 2 \\ \times 2 \\ \hline \end{array}$
8. $\begin{array}{r} 4 \\ \times 2 \\ \hline \end{array}$
9. $\begin{array}{r} 3 \\ \times 2 \\ \hline \end{array}$
10. $\begin{array}{r} 2 \\ \times 1 \\ \hline \end{array}$
11. $\begin{array}{r} 2 \\ \times 5 \\ \hline \end{array}$
12. $\begin{array}{r} 5 \\ \times 2 \\ \hline \end{array}$

13. $\begin{array}{r} 0 \\ \times 2 \\ \hline \end{array}$
14. $\begin{array}{r} 2 \\ \times 3 \\ \hline \end{array}$
15. $\begin{array}{r} 3 \\ \times 5 \\ \hline \end{array}$
16. $\begin{array}{r} 0 \\ \times 1 \\ \hline \end{array}$
17. $\begin{array}{r} 4 \\ \times 2 \\ \hline \end{array}$
18. $\begin{array}{r} 1 \\ \times 0 \\ \hline \end{array}$

19. $\begin{array}{r} 0 \\ \times 3 \\ \hline \end{array}$
20. $\begin{array}{r} 2 \\ \times 4 \\ \hline \end{array}$
21. $\begin{array}{r} 1 \\ \times 4 \\ \hline \end{array}$
22. $\begin{array}{r} 5 \\ \times 1 \\ \hline \end{array}$
23. $\begin{array}{r} 0 \\ \times 0 \\ \hline \end{array}$
24. $\begin{array}{r} 3 \\ \times 1 \\ \hline \end{array}$

25. $\begin{array}{r} 3 \\ \times 4 \\ \hline \end{array}$
26. $\begin{array}{r} 3 \\ \times 3 \\ \hline \end{array}$
27. $\begin{array}{r} 3 \\ \times 1 \\ \hline \end{array}$

Multiplication with Factors 0 to 5

Total Problems:	27
Problems Correct:	_____

Solve each problem.

Hooray for Math!

1. 4
    × 0

2. 5
    × 0

3. 5
    × 4

4. 3
    × 3

5. 5
    × 1

6. 3
    × 2

7. 4
    × 2

8. 5
    × 1

9. 3
    × 4

10. 4
    × 3

11. 3
    × 0

12. 3
    × 5

13. 4
    × 4

14. 4
    × 3

15. 3
    × 3

16. 4
    × 5

17. 4
    × 0

18. 5
    × 5

19. 5
    × 2

20. 5
    × 3

21. 3
    × 1

22. 5
    × 1

23. 3
    × 0

24. 4
    × 1

25. 3
    × 2

26. 4
    × 3

27. 3
    × 3

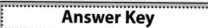

Worksheet 1 (page 4)

Name _____ Date _____

Sums to 6

Total Problems: 27
Problems Correct: _____

Solve each problem.

Jump to It!

#		#		#		#		#		#	
1.	$\begin{array}{r}5\\+1\\\hline 6\end{array}$	2.	$\begin{array}{r}6\\+0\\\hline 6\end{array}$	3.	$\begin{array}{r}2\\+3\\\hline 5\end{array}$	4.	$\begin{array}{r}0\\+2\\\hline 2\end{array}$	5.	$\begin{array}{r}2\\+1\\\hline 3\end{array}$	6.	$\begin{array}{r}3\\+0\\\hline 3\end{array}$
7.	$\begin{array}{r}1\\+2\\\hline 3\end{array}$	8.	$\begin{array}{r}3\\+2\\\hline 5\end{array}$	9.	$\begin{array}{r}3\\+0\\\hline 3\end{array}$	10.	$\begin{array}{r}3\\+2\\\hline 5\end{array}$	11.	$\begin{array}{r}1\\+3\\\hline 4\end{array}$	12.	$\begin{array}{r}1\\+4\\\hline 5\end{array}$
13.	$\begin{array}{r}1\\+5\\\hline 6\end{array}$	14.	$\begin{array}{r}0\\+0\\\hline 0\end{array}$	15.	$\begin{array}{r}2\\+4\\\hline 6\end{array}$	16.	$\begin{array}{r}0\\+5\\\hline 5\end{array}$	17.	$\begin{array}{r}2\\+2\\\hline 4\end{array}$	18.	$\begin{array}{r}2\\+3\\\hline 5\end{array}$
19.	$\begin{array}{r}3\\+3\\\hline 6\end{array}$	20.	$\begin{array}{r}4\\+1\\\hline 5\end{array}$	21.	$\begin{array}{r}1\\+1\\\hline 2\end{array}$	22.	$\begin{array}{r}2\\+4\\\hline 6\end{array}$	23.	$\begin{array}{r}0\\+6\\\hline 6\end{array}$	24.	$\begin{array}{r}4\\+2\\\hline 6\end{array}$
25.	$\begin{array}{r}5\\+0\\\hline 5\end{array}$	26.	$\begin{array}{r}3\\+1\\\hline 4\end{array}$	27.	$\begin{array}{r}1\\+1\\\hline 2\end{array}$						

CD-104318 • © Carson-Dellosa

Worksheet 2 (page 5)

Name _____ Date _____

Sums to 6

Total Problems: 27
Problems Correct: _____

Solve each problem.

You Can Do It!

1. 2 + 4 = **6**
2. 1 + 5 = **6**
3. 2 + 3 = **5**
4. 0 + 0 = **0**
5. 2 + 1 = **3**
6. 1 + 1 = **2**
7. 3 + 1 = **4**
8. 5 + 1 = **6**
9. 4 + 1 = **5**
10. 0 + 2 = **2**
11. 0 + 5 = **5**
12. 2 + 2 = **4**
13. 5 + 1 = **6**
14. 3 + 2 = **5**
15. 4 + 0 = **4**
16. 1 + 4 = **5**
17. 4 + 2 = **6**
18. 0 + 4 = **4**
19. 2 + 2 = **4**
20. 1 + 3 = **4**
21. 3 + 0 = **3**
22. 6 + 0 = **6**
23. 2 + 1 = **3**
24. 0 + 6 = **6**
25. 1 + 2 = **3**
26. 0 + 3 = **3**
27. 2 + 3 = **5**

CD-104318 • © Carson-Dellosa

Worksheet 3 (page 6)

Name _____ Date _____

Sums to 7

Total Problems: 27
Problems Correct: _____

Solve each problem.

Have Fun with Addition!

#		#		#		#		#		#	
1.	$\begin{array}{r}2\\+1\\\hline 3\end{array}$	2.	$\begin{array}{r}1\\+6\\\hline 7\end{array}$	3.	$\begin{array}{r}4\\+3\\\hline 7\end{array}$	4.	$\begin{array}{r}6\\+0\\\hline 6\end{array}$	5.	$\begin{array}{r}5\\+2\\\hline 7\end{array}$	6.	$\begin{array}{r}7\\+0\\\hline 7\end{array}$
7.	$\begin{array}{r}2\\+2\\\hline 4\end{array}$	8.	$\begin{array}{r}2\\+5\\\hline 7\end{array}$	9.	$\begin{array}{r}2\\+4\\\hline 6\end{array}$	10.	$\begin{array}{r}3\\+1\\\hline 4\end{array}$	11.	$\begin{array}{r}1\\+2\\\hline 3\end{array}$	12.	$\begin{array}{r}3\\+2\\\hline 5\end{array}$
13.	$\begin{array}{r}4\\+2\\\hline 6\end{array}$	14.	$\begin{array}{r}3\\+3\\\hline 6\end{array}$	15.	$\begin{array}{r}5\\+0\\\hline 5\end{array}$	16.	$\begin{array}{r}0\\+5\\\hline 5\end{array}$	17.	$\begin{array}{r}2\\+0\\\hline 2\end{array}$	18.	$\begin{array}{r}3\\+4\\\hline 7\end{array}$
19.	$\begin{array}{r}6\\+1\\\hline 7\end{array}$	20.	$\begin{array}{r}5\\+1\\\hline 6\end{array}$	21.	$\begin{array}{r}0\\+0\\\hline 0\end{array}$	22.	$\begin{array}{r}3\\+4\\\hline 7\end{array}$	23.	$\begin{array}{r}4\\+1\\\hline 5\end{array}$	24.	$\begin{array}{r}5\\+1\\\hline 6\end{array}$
25.	$\begin{array}{r}0\\+7\\\hline 7\end{array}$	26.	$\begin{array}{r}2\\+3\\\hline 5\end{array}$	27.	$\begin{array}{r}1\\+5\\\hline 6\end{array}$						

CD-104318 • © Carson-Dellosa

Worksheet 4 (page 7)

Name _____ Date _____

Sums to 10

Total Problems: 27
Problems Correct: _____

Solve each problem.

Fly High with Addition!

#		#		#		#		#		#	
1.	$\begin{array}{r}3\\+3\\\hline 6\end{array}$	2.	$\begin{array}{r}7\\+3\\\hline 10\end{array}$	3.	$\begin{array}{r}0\\+3\\\hline 3\end{array}$	4.	$\begin{array}{r}6\\+2\\\hline 8\end{array}$	5.	$\begin{array}{r}0\\+9\\\hline 9\end{array}$	6.	$\begin{array}{r}3\\+6\\\hline 9\end{array}$
7.	$\begin{array}{r}8\\+0\\\hline 8\end{array}$	8.	$\begin{array}{r}1\\+4\\\hline 5\end{array}$	9.	$\begin{array}{r}1\\+8\\\hline 9\end{array}$	10.	$\begin{array}{r}2\\+5\\\hline 7\end{array}$	11.	$\begin{array}{r}5\\+5\\\hline 10\end{array}$	12.	$\begin{array}{r}2\\+3\\\hline 5\end{array}$
13.	$\begin{array}{r}5\\+1\\\hline 6\end{array}$	14.	$\begin{array}{r}6\\+1\\\hline 7\end{array}$	15.	$\begin{array}{r}3\\+5\\\hline 8\end{array}$	16.	$\begin{array}{r}2\\+7\\\hline 9\end{array}$	17.	$\begin{array}{r}5\\+4\\\hline 9\end{array}$	18.	$\begin{array}{r}5\\+2\\\hline 7\end{array}$
19.	$\begin{array}{r}6\\+8\\\hline 10\end{array}$	20.	$\begin{array}{r}5\\+3\\\hline 8\end{array}$	21.	$\begin{array}{r}1\\+2\\\hline 3\end{array}$	22.	$\begin{array}{r}4\\+4\\\hline 8\end{array}$	23.	$\begin{array}{r}2\\+2\\\hline 4\end{array}$	24.	$\begin{array}{r}10\\+0\\\hline 10\end{array}$
25.	$\begin{array}{r}9\\+1\\\hline 10\end{array}$	26.	$\begin{array}{r}5\\+0\\\hline 5\end{array}$	27.	$\begin{array}{r}6\\+4\\\hline 10\end{array}$						

CD-104318 • © Carson-Dellosa

CD-104318 • © Carson-Dellosa

Panel 1 (page 8)

Name _____ Date _____

Sums to 10

Total Problems:	27
Problems Correct:	_____

Solve each problem.

Practice Makes Perfect!

1. $\begin{array}{r} 7 \\ +2 \\ \hline 9 \end{array}$	2. $\begin{array}{r} 5 \\ +5 \\ \hline 10 \end{array}$	3. $\begin{array}{r} 2 \\ +6 \\ \hline 8 \end{array}$	4. $\begin{array}{r} 2 \\ +5 \\ \hline 7 \end{array}$	5. $\begin{array}{r} 5 \\ +0 \\ \hline 5 \end{array}$	6. $\begin{array}{r} 3 \\ +6 \\ \hline 9 \end{array}$
7. $\begin{array}{r} 2 \\ +8 \\ \hline 10 \end{array}$	8. $\begin{array}{r} 9 \\ +1 \\ \hline 10 \end{array}$	9. $\begin{array}{r} 4 \\ +3 \\ \hline 7 \end{array}$	10. $\begin{array}{r} 4 \\ +5 \\ \hline 9 \end{array}$	11. $\begin{array}{r} 3 \\ +3 \\ \hline 6 \end{array}$	12. $\begin{array}{r} 5 \\ +4 \\ \hline 9 \end{array}$
13. $\begin{array}{r} 6 \\ +1 \\ \hline 7 \end{array}$	14. $\begin{array}{r} 3 \\ +1 \\ \hline 4 \end{array}$	15. $\begin{array}{r} 2 \\ +2 \\ \hline 4 \end{array}$	16. $\begin{array}{r} 2 \\ +7 \\ \hline 9 \end{array}$	17. $\begin{array}{r} 3 \\ +5 \\ \hline 8 \end{array}$	18. $\begin{array}{r} 3 \\ +7 \\ \hline 10 \end{array}$
19. $\begin{array}{r} 1 \\ +7 \\ \hline 8 \end{array}$	20. $\begin{array}{r} 4 \\ +2 \\ \hline 6 \end{array}$	21. $\begin{array}{r} 3 \\ +2 \\ \hline 5 \end{array}$	22. $\begin{array}{r} 1 \\ +0 \\ \hline 1 \end{array}$	23. $\begin{array}{r} 5 \\ +1 \\ \hline 6 \end{array}$	24. $\begin{array}{r} 1 \\ +1 \\ \hline 2 \end{array}$
25. $\begin{array}{r} 8 \\ +1 \\ \hline 9 \end{array}$	26. $\begin{array}{r} 0 \\ +7 \\ \hline 7 \end{array}$	27. $\begin{array}{r} 6 \\ +2 \\ \hline 8 \end{array}$			

8   CD-104318 • © Carson-Dellosa

Panel 2 (page 9)

Name _____ Date _____

Sums to 10

Total Problems:	27
Problems Correct:	_____

Solve each problem.

Way to Give a Royal Effort!

1. $1 + 6 = 7$	2. $0 + 1 = 1$	3. $4 + 5 = 9$
4. $4 + 2 = 6$	5. $3 + 6 = 9$	6. $1 + 3 = 4$
7. $7 + 2 = 9$	8. $3 + 2 = 5$	9. $8 + 2 = 10$
10. $4 + 3 = 7$	11. $6 + 3 = 9$	12. $5 + 3 = 8$
13. $1 + 3 = 4$	14. $4 + 6 = 10$	15. $2 + 0 = 2$
16. $5 + 1 = 6$	17. $5 + 2 = 7$	18. $6 + 4 = 10$
19. $5 + 5 = 10$	20. $2 + 1 = 3$	21. $2 + 6 = 8$
22. $4 + 1 = 5$	23. $0 + 4 = 4$	
24. $3 + 7 = 10$	25. $6 + 2 = 8$	
26. $9 + 0 = 9$	27. $2 + 8 = 10$	

CD-104318 • © Carson-Dellosa   9

Panel 3 (page 10)

Name _____ Date _____

Differences from 6 or Less

Total Problems:	27
Problems Correct:	_____

Solve each problem.

Sss-ubtracting!

1. $\begin{array}{r} 6 \\ -0 \\ \hline 6 \end{array}$	2. $\begin{array}{r} 4 \\ -1 \\ \hline 3 \end{array}$	3. $\begin{array}{r} 0 \\ -0 \\ \hline 0 \end{array}$	4. $\begin{array}{r} 6 \\ -3 \\ \hline 3 \end{array}$	5. $\begin{array}{r} 6 \\ -5 \\ \hline 1 \end{array}$	6. $\begin{array}{r} 3 \\ -3 \\ \hline 0 \end{array}$
7. $\begin{array}{r} 6 \\ -5 \\ \hline 1 \end{array}$	8. $\begin{array}{r} 4 \\ -3 \\ \hline 1 \end{array}$	9. $\begin{array}{r} 4 \\ -1 \\ \hline 3 \end{array}$	10. $\begin{array}{r} 6 \\ -4 \\ \hline 2 \end{array}$	11. $\begin{array}{r} 5 \\ -0 \\ \hline 5 \end{array}$	12. $\begin{array}{r} 4 \\ -0 \\ \hline 4 \end{array}$
13. $\begin{array}{r} 5 \\ -0 \\ \hline 5 \end{array}$	14. $\begin{array}{r} 5 \\ -1 \\ \hline 4 \end{array}$	15. $\begin{array}{r} 4 \\ -2 \\ \hline 2 \end{array}$	16. $\begin{array}{r} 0 \\ -0 \\ \hline 0 \end{array}$	17. $\begin{array}{r} 2 \\ -1 \\ \hline 1 \end{array}$	18. $\begin{array}{r} 3 \\ -2 \\ \hline 1 \end{array}$
19. $\begin{array}{r} 1 \\ -1 \\ \hline 0 \end{array}$	20. $\begin{array}{r} 2 \\ -0 \\ \hline 2 \end{array}$	21. $\begin{array}{r} 6 \\ -1 \\ \hline 5 \end{array}$	22. $\begin{array}{r} 5 \\ -5 \\ \hline 0 \end{array}$	23. $\begin{array}{r} 5 \\ -4 \\ \hline 1 \end{array}$	24. $\begin{array}{r} 6 \\ -3 \\ \hline 3 \end{array}$
25. $\begin{array}{r} 4 \\ -4 \\ \hline 0 \end{array}$	26. $\begin{array}{r} 6 \\ -6 \\ \hline 0 \end{array}$	27. $\begin{array}{r} 5 \\ -4 \\ \hline 1 \end{array}$			

10   CD-104318 • © Carson-Dellosa

Panel 4 (page 11)

Name _____ Date _____

Differences from 6 or Less

Total Problems:	27
Problems Correct:	_____

Solve each problem.

Discover the Answers!

1. $6 - 5 = 1$	2. $5 - 4 = 1$	3. $1 - 0 = 1$
4. $2 - 2 = 0$	5. $1 - 1 = 0$	6. $6 - 2 = 4$
7. $5 - 3 = 2$	8. $3 - 2 = 1$	9. $6 - 2 = 4$
10. $3 - 1 = 2$	11. $6 - 6 = 0$	12. $4 - 4 = 0$
13. $2 - 0 = 2$	14. $4 - 3 = 1$	15. $6 - 0 = 6$
16. $2 - 0 = 2$	17. $5 - 0 = 5$	18. $5 - 5 = 0$
19. $6 - 3 = 3$	20. $5 - 1 = 4$	21. $6 - 4 = 2$
22. $6 - 3 = 3$	23. $5 - 2 = 3$	
24. $3 - 0 = 3$	25. $5 - 2 = 3$	
26. $3 - 1 = 2$	27. $4 - 1 = 3$	

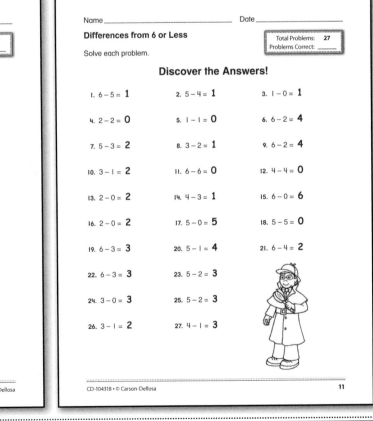

CD-104318 • © Carson-Dellosa   11

Answer Key

Differences from 7 or Less

Solve each problem.

Total Problems: 27
Problems Correct: _____

Busy as a Bee!

1. 5 − 2 = 3
2. 6 − 2 = 4
3. 0 − 0 = 0
4. 7 − 2 = 5
5. 6 − 4 = 2
6. 2 − 1 = 1

7. 7 − 4 = 3
8. 7 − 3 = 4
9. 4 − 4 = 0
10. 3 − 2 = 1
11. 6 − 1 = 5
12. 4 − 1 = 3

13. 7 − 5 = 2
14. 3 − 0 = 3
15. 6 − 3 = 3
16. 5 − 3 = 2
17. 7 − 5 = 2
18. 4 − 2 = 2

19. 5 − 4 = 1
20. 6 − 5 = 1
21. 7 − 6 = 1
22. 7 − 0 = 7
23. 7 − 2 = 5
24. 5 − 0 = 5

25. 3 − 3 = 0
26. 7 − 1 = 6
27. 7 − 4 = 3

12   CD-104318 • © Carson-Dellosa

Differences from 7 or Less

Solve each problem.

Total Problems: 27
Problems Correct: _____

Hard at Work!

1. 6 − 4 = 2
2. 4 − 4 = 0
3. 7 − 2 = 5
4. 3 − 2 = 1
5. 7 − 2 = 5
6. 7 − 3 = 4
7. 2 − 2 = 0
8. 6 − 3 = 3
9. 7 − 0 = 7
10. 7 − 4 = 3
11. 7 − 1 = 6
12. 3 − 0 = 3
13. 3 − 3 = 0
14. 5 − 0 = 5
15. 2 − 2 = 0
16. 8 − 4 = 4
17. 6 − 5 = 1
18. 4 − 0 = 4
19. 5 − 2 = 3
20. 5 − 0 = 5
21. 5 − 1 = 4
22. 6 − 4 = 2
23. 4 − 3 = 1
24. 3 − 2 = 1
25. 6 − 2 = 4
26. 0 − 0 = 0
27. 7 − 6 = 1

CD-104318 • © Carson-Dellosa   13

Differences from 8 or Less

Solve each problem.

Total Problems: 27
Problems Correct: _____

You're Doing Grrr-eat!

1. 6 − 2 = 4
2. 6 − 5 = 1
3. 8 − 3 = 5
4. 5 − 3 = 2
5. 7 − 7 = 0
6. 6 − 3 = 3

7. 6 − 4 = 2
8. 8 − 7 = 1
9. 7 − 4 = 3
10. 8 − 6 = 2
11. 7 − 1 = 6
12. 7 − 6 = 1

13. 8 − 1 = 7
14. 5 − 4 = 1
15. 5 − 2 = 3
16. 4 − 2 = 2
17. 6 − 0 = 6
18. 4 − 2 = 2

19. 8 − 0 = 8
20. 6 − 6 = 0
21. 7 − 2 = 5
22. 8 − 2 = 6
23. 8 − 5 = 3
24. 8 − 4 = 4

25. 5 − 5 = 0
26. 8 − 5 = 3
27. 8 − 4 = 4

14   CD-104318 • © Carson-Dellosa

Differences from 8 or Less

Solve each problem.

Total Problems: 27
Problems Correct: _____

Keep It Up!

1. 7 − 0 = 7
2. 4 − 2 = 2
3. 8 − 2 = 6
4. 8 − 3 = 5
5. 8 − 0 = 8
6. 7 − 3 = 4
7. 8 − 5 = 3
8. 2 − 2 = 0
9. 6 − 4 = 2
10. 5 − 0 = 5
11. 5 − 3 = 2
12. 6 − 6 = 0
13. 5 − 4 = 1
14. 7 − 3 = 4
15. 6 − 3 = 3
16. 8 − 4 = 4
17. 6 − 4 = 2
18. 7 − 2 = 5
19. 8 − 3 = 5
20. 7 − 6 = 1
21. 3 − 3 = 0
22. 8 − 7 = 1
23. 7 − 4 = 3
24. 8 − 6 = 2
25. 7 − 1 = 6
26. 5 − 5 = 0
27. 7 − 6 = 1

CD-104318 • © Carson-Dellosa   15

106   CD-104318 • © Carson-Dellosa

Page 16

Name _____ Date _____

Differences from 9 or Less

Total Problems: 27
Problems Correct: _____

Solve each problem.

Up, Up, and Away with Subtracting!

1. $9 - 3 = 6$	2. $9 - 5 = 4$	3. $7 - 3 = 4$	4. $8 - 5 = 3$	5. $8 - 2 = 6$	6. $9 - 6 = 3$
7. $9 - 2 = 7$	8. $8 - 1 = 7$	9. $7 - 5 = 2$	10. $7 - 2 = 5$	11. $6 - 5 = 1$	12. $9 - 9 = 0$
13. $8 - 8 = 0$	14. $8 - 6 = 2$	15. $5 - 4 = 1$	16. $6 - 2 = 4$	17. $7 - 6 = 1$	18. $9 - 4 = 5$
19. $9 - 0 = 9$	20. $8 - 3 = 5$	21. $7 - 1 = 6$	22. $9 - 6 = 3$	23. $5 - 3 = 2$	24. $7 - 4 = 3$
25. $9 - 1 = 8$	26. $8 - 4 = 4$	27. $9 - 8 = 1$			

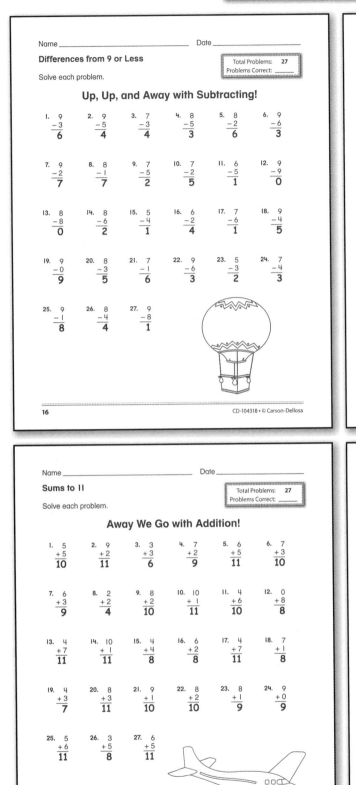

16   CD-104318 • © Carson-Dellosa

Page 17

Name _____ Date _____

Differences from 9 or Less

Total Problems: 27
Problems Correct: _____

Solve each problem.

Stretch Your Brain!

1. $7 - 4 = 3$	2. $9 - 6 = 3$	3. $8 - 8 = 0$
4. $8 - 3 = 5$	5. $7 - 0 = 7$	6. $4 - 4 = 0$
7. $8 - 1 = 7$	8. $9 - 2 = 7$	9. $9 - 5 = 4$
10. $7 - 5 = 2$	11. $8 - 2 = 6$	12. $9 - 3 = 6$
13. $7 - 3 = 4$	14. $9 - 0 = 9$	15. $9 - 1 = 8$
16. $8 - 4 = 4$	17. $6 - 5 = 1$	18. $5 - 4 = 1$
19. $8 - 3 = 5$	20. $9 - 9 = 0$	21. $5 - 3 = 2$
22. $9 - 4 = 5$	23. $7 - 2 = 5$	
24. $8 - 6 = 2$	25. $9 - 2 = 7$	
26. $6 - 2 = 4$	27. $7 - 6 = 1$	

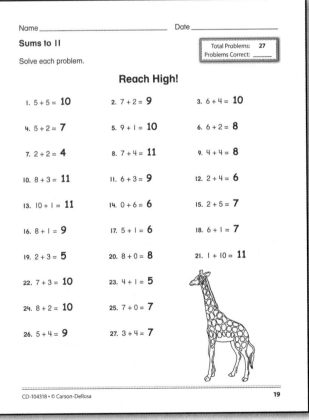

CD-104318 • © Carson-Dellosa   17

Page 18

Name _____ Date _____

Sums to 11

Total Problems: 27
Problems Correct: _____

Solve each problem.

Away We Go with Addition!

1. $5 + 5 = 10$	2. $9 + 2 = 11$	3. $3 + 3 = 6$	4. $7 + 2 = 9$	5. $6 + 5 = 11$	6. $7 + 3 = 10$
7. $6 + 3 = 9$	8. $2 + 2 = 4$	9. $8 + 2 = 10$	10. $10 + 1 = 11$	11. $4 + 6 = 10$	12. $0 + 8 = 8$
13. $4 + 7 = 11$	14. $10 + 1 = 11$	15. $4 + 4 = 8$	16. $6 + 2 = 8$	17. $4 + 7 = 11$	18. $7 + 1 = 8$
19. $4 + 3 = 7$	20. $8 + 3 = 11$	21. $9 + 1 = 10$	22. $8 + 2 = 10$	23. $8 + 1 = 9$	24. $9 + 0 = 9$
25. $5 + 6 = 11$	26. $3 + 5 = 8$	27. $6 + 5 = 11$			

18   CD-104318 • © Carson-Dellosa

Page 19

Name _____ Date _____

Sums to 11

Total Problems: 27
Problems Correct: _____

Solve each problem.

Reach High!

1. $5 + 5 = 10$	2. $7 + 2 = 9$	3. $6 + 4 = 10$
4. $5 + 2 = 7$	5. $9 + 1 = 10$	6. $6 + 2 = 8$
7. $2 + 2 = 4$	8. $7 + 4 = 11$	9. $4 + 4 = 8$
10. $8 + 3 = 11$	11. $6 + 3 = 9$	12. $2 + 4 = 6$
13. $10 + 1 = 11$	14. $0 + 6 = 6$	15. $2 + 5 = 7$
16. $8 + 1 = 9$	17. $5 + 1 = 6$	18. $6 + 1 = 7$
19. $2 + 3 = 5$	20. $8 + 0 = 8$	21. $1 + 10 = 11$
22. $7 + 3 = 10$	23. $4 + 1 = 5$	
24. $8 + 2 = 10$	25. $7 + 0 = 7$	
26. $5 + 4 = 9$	27. $3 + 4 = 7$	

CD-104318 • © Carson-Dellosa   19

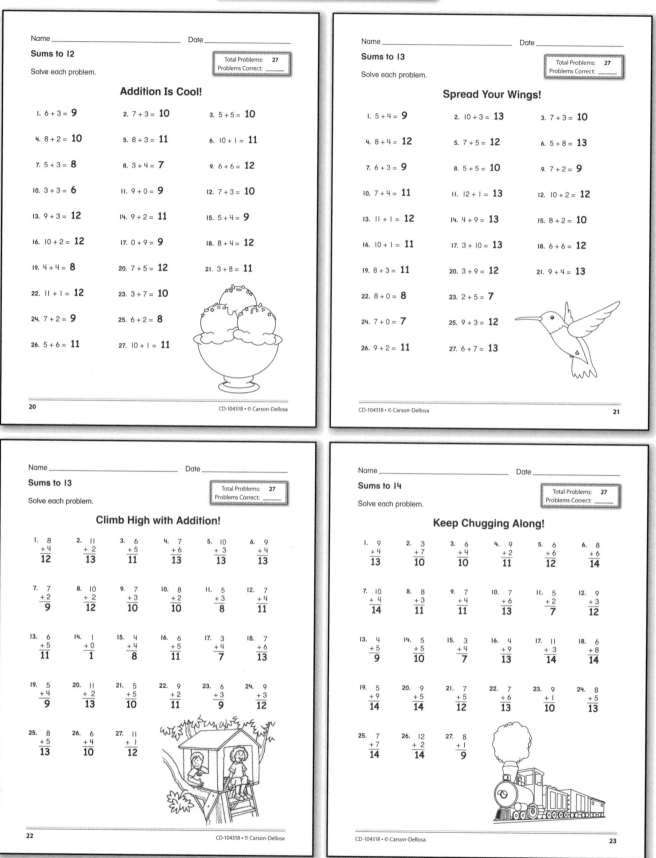

Name _____ Date _____

Sums to 12

Solve each problem.

Total Problems: **27**
Problems Correct: _____

Addition Is Cool!

1. 6 + 3 = **9**   2. 7 + 3 = **10**   3. 5 + 5 = **10**

4. 8 + 2 = **10**   5. 8 + 3 = **11**   6. 10 + 1 = **11**

7. 5 + 3 = **8**   8. 3 + 4 = **7**   9. 6 + 6 = **12**

10. 3 + 3 = **6**   11. 9 + 0 = **9**   12. 7 + 3 = **10**

13. 9 + 3 = **12**   14. 9 + 2 = **11**   15. 5 + 4 = **9**

16. 10 + 2 = **12**   17. 0 + 9 = **9**   18. 8 + 4 = **12**

19. 4 + 4 = **8**   20. 7 + 5 = **12**   21. 3 + 8 = **11**

22. 11 + 1 = **12**   23. 3 + 7 = **10**

24. 7 + 2 = **9**   25. 6 + 2 = **8**

26. 5 + 6 = **11**   27. 10 + 1 = **11**

CD-104318 • © Carson-Dellosa

Name _____ Date _____

Sums to 13

Solve each problem.

Total Problems: **27**
Problems Correct: _____

Spread Your Wings!

1. 5 + 4 = **9**   2. 10 + 3 = **13**   3. 7 + 3 = **10**

4. 8 + 4 = **12**   5. 7 + 5 = **12**   6. 5 + 8 = **13**

7. 6 + 3 = **9**   8. 5 + 5 = **10**   9. 7 + 2 = **9**

10. 7 + 4 = **11**   11. 12 + 1 = **13**   12. 10 + 2 = **12**

13. 11 + 1 = **12**   14. 4 + 9 = **13**   15. 8 + 2 = **10**

16. 10 + 1 = **11**   17. 3 + 10 = **13**   18. 6 + 6 = **12**

19. 8 + 3 = **11**   20. 3 + 9 = **12**   21. 9 + 4 = **13**

22. 8 + 0 = **8**   23. 2 + 5 = **7**

24. 7 + 0 = **7**   25. 9 + 3 = **12**

26. 9 + 2 = **11**   27. 6 + 7 = **13**

CD-104318 • © Carson-Dellosa

Name _____ Date _____

Sums to 13

Solve each problem.

Total Problems: **27**
Problems Correct: _____

Climb High with Addition!

1. 8 + 4 = **12**   2. 11 + 2 = **13**   3. 6 + 5 = **11**   4. 7 + 6 = **13**   5. 10 + 3 = **13**   6. 9 + 4 = **13**

7. 7 + 2 = **9**   8. 10 + 2 = **12**   9. 7 + 3 = **10**   10. 8 + 2 = **10**   11. 5 + 3 = **8**   12. 7 + 4 = **11**

13. 6 + 5 = **11**   14. 1 + 0 = **1**   15. 4 + 4 = **8**   16. 6 + 5 = **11**   17. 3 + 4 = **7**   18. 7 + 6 = **13**

19. 5 + 4 = **9**   20. 11 + 2 = **13**   21. 5 + 5 = **10**   22. 9 + 2 = **11**   23. 6 + 3 = **9**   24. 9 + 3 = **12**

25. 8 + 5 = **13**   26. 6 + 4 = **10**   27. 11 + 1 = **12**

CD-104318 • © Carson-Dellosa

Name _____ Date _____

Sums to 14

Solve each problem.

Total Problems: **27**
Problems Correct: _____

Keep Chugging Along!

1. 9 + 4 = **13**   2. 3 + 7 = **10**   3. 6 + 4 = **10**   4. 9 + 2 = **11**   5. 6 + 6 = **12**   6. 8 + 6 = **14**

7. 10 + 4 = **14**   8. 8 + 3 = **11**   9. 7 + 4 = **11**   10. 7 + 6 = **13**   11. 5 + 2 = **7**   12. 9 + 3 = **12**

13. 4 + 5 = **9**   14. 5 + 5 = **10**   15. 3 + 4 = **7**   16. 4 + 9 = **13**   17. 11 + 3 = **14**   18. 6 + 8 = **14**

19. 5 + 9 = **14**   20. 9 + 5 = **14**   21. 7 + 5 = **12**   22. 7 + 6 = **13**   23. 9 + 1 = **10**   24. 8 + 5 = **13**

25. 7 + 7 = **14**   26. 12 + 2 = **14**   27. 8 + 1 = **9**

CD-104318 • © Carson-Dellosa

CD-104318 • © Carson-Dellosa

You're Doing Swimmingly!

Name _____ Date _____

Sums to 14

Total Problems: 27
Problems Correct: _____

Solve each problem.

1. 8 + 3 = 11
2. 9 + 5 = 14
3. 3 + 8 = 11
4. 2 + 9 = 11
5. 6 + 8 = 14
6. 7 + 5 = 12

7. 1 + 9 = 10
8. 8 + 5 = 13
9. 13 + 1 = 14
10. 7 + 3 = 10
11. 6 + 5 = 11
12. 4 + 9 = 13

13. 4 + 6 = 10
14. 9 + 3 = 12
15. 8 + 2 = 10
16. 7 + 7 = 14
17. 5 + 8 = 13
18. 4 + 8 = 12

19. 8 + 4 = 12
20. 5 + 9 = 14
21. 5 + 7 = 12
22. 10 + 4 = 14
23. 5 + 6 = 11
24. 4 + 7 = 11

25. 5 + 5 = 10
26. 12 + 1 = 13
27. 9 + 5 = 14

24   CD-104318 • © Carson-Dellosa

Remember Your Addition!

Name _____ Date _____

Sums to 14

Total Problems: 27
Problems Correct: _____

Solve each problem.

1. 8 + 2 = 10
2. 10 + 4 = 14
3. 2 + 9 = 11
4. 9 + 1 = 10
5. 4 + 9 = 13
6. 5 + 7 = 12

7. 6 + 6 = 12
8. 8 + 3 = 11
9. 9 + 5 = 14
10. 7 + 5 = 12
11. 7 + 6 = 13
12. 11 + 0 = 11

13. 5 + 9 = 14
14. 3 + 8 = 11
15. 4 + 8 = 12
16. 3 + 7 = 10
17. 8 + 4 = 12
18. 6 + 5 = 11

19. 5 + 8 = 13
20. 3 + 9 = 12
21. 8 + 5 = 13
22. 9 + 4 = 13
23. 6 + 8 = 14
24. 6 + 7 = 13

25. 4 + 7 = 11
26. 5 + 6 = 11
27. 10 + 0 = 10

CD-104318 • © Carson-Dellosa   25

Moo-ving Right Along!

Name _____ Date _____

Sums from 10 to 14

Total Problems: 27
Problems Correct: _____

Solve each problem.

1. 8 + 4 = 12
2. 13 + 1 = 14
3. 7 + 7 = 14
4. 9 + 5 = 14
5. 14 + 0 = 14
6. 2 + 9 = 11
7. 6 + 8 = 14
8. 6 + 5 = 11
9. 9 + 3 = 12
10. 1 + 9 = 10
11. 4 + 7 = 11
12. 5 + 8 = 13
13. 4 + 8 = 12
14. 8 + 3 = 11
15. 10 + 2 = 12
16. 6 + 6 = 12
17. 7 + 3 = 10
18. 7 + 4 = 11
19. 7 + 5 = 12
20. 7 + 6 = 13
21. 9 + 2 = 11
22. 2 + 8 = 10
23. 5 + 9 = 14
24. 3 + 7 = 10
25. 5 + 6 = 11
26. 3 + 8 = 11
27. 9 + 4 = 13

26   CD-104318 • © Carson-Dellosa

Give It Your All!

Name _____ Date _____

Sums to 15

Total Problems: 27
Problems Correct: _____

Solve each problem.

1. 8 + 4 = 12
2. 7 + 5 = 12
3. 10 + 5 = 15
4. 7 + 8 = 15
5. 5 + 6 = 11
6. 7 + 6 = 13

7. 9 + 2 = 11
8. 6 + 3 = 9
9. 4 + 5 = 9
10. 8 + 6 = 14
11. 7 + 3 = 10
12. 6 + 6 = 12

13. 9 + 5 = 14
14. 9 + 1 = 10
15. 8 + 3 = 11
16. 5 + 5 = 10
17. 9 + 4 = 13
18. 8 + 2 = 10

19. 6 + 9 = 15
20. 8 + 7 = 15
21. 8 + 5 = 13
22. 11 + 2 = 13
23. 9 + 3 = 12
24. 7 + 4 = 11

25. 9 + 6 = 15
26. 6 + 7 = 13
27. 3 + 8 = 11

CD-104318 • © Carson-Dellosa   27

Page 28 — Sums to 16

Name _____ Date _____

Sums to 16

Total Problems: 27
Problems Correct: _____

Solve each problem.

Mighty Math!

1. $7 + 7 = 14$
2. $6 + 6 = 12$
3. $9 + 3 = 12$
4. $9 + 6 = 15$
5. $6 + 5 = 11$
6. $12 + 4 = 16$
7. $9 + 7 = 16$
8. $7 + 3 = 10$
9. $8 + 3 = 11$
10. $6 + 7 = 13$
11. $8 + 8 = 16$
12. $7 + 5 = 12$
13. $6 + 2 = 8$
14. $7 + 6 = 13$
15. $9 + 2 = 11$
16. $7 + 8 = 15$
17. $15 + 1 = 16$
18. $9 + 4 = 13$
19. $9 + 5 = 14$
20. $8 + 4 = 12$
21. $5 + 5 = 10$
22. $8 + 3 = 11$
23. $7 + 2 = 9$
24. $8 + 2 = 10$
25. $6 + 4 = 10$
26. $11 + 4 = 15$
27. $9 + 1 = 10$

28 CD-104318 • © Carson-Dellosa

Page 29 — Sums to 17

Name _____ Date _____

Sums to 17

Total Problems: 27
Problems Correct: _____

Solve each problem.

Spring into Addition!

1. $8 + 2 = 10$
2. $9 + 8 = 17$
3. $6 + 4 = 10$
4. $9 + 6 = 15$
5. $6 + 5 = 11$
6. $8 + 8 = 16$
7. $7 + 6 = 13$
8. $15 + 2 = 17$
9. $9 + 2 = 11$
10. $7 + 5 = 12$
11. $5 + 5 = 10$
12. $5 + 6 = 11$
13. $7 + 4 = 11$
14. $6 + 6 = 12$
15. $6 + 8 = 14$
16. $7 + 8 = 15$
17. $9 + 4 = 13$
18. $8 + 7 = 15$
19. $8 + 6 = 14$
20. $8 + 9 = 17$
21. $9 + 1 = 10$
22. $7 + 3 = 10$
23. $9 + 3 = 12$
24. $11 + 6 = 17$
25. $10 + 7 = 17$
26. $7 + 2 = 9$
27. $5 + 8 = 13$

CD-104318 • © Carson-Dellosa 29

Page 30 — Sums to 18

Name _____ Date _____

Sums to 18

Total Problems: 27
Problems Correct: _____

Solve each problem.

Addition Is a Blast!

1. $9 + 6 = 15$
2. $10 + 8 = 18$
3. $8 + 5 = 13$
4. $6 + 7 = 13$
5. $5 + 5 = 10$
6. $6 + 4 = 10$
7. $9 + 7 = 16$
8. $12 + 6 = 18$
9. $5 + 6 = 11$
10. $9 + 9 = 18$
11. $6 + 3 = 9$
12. $7 + 4 = 11$
13. $8 + 6 = 14$
14. $7 + 6 = 13$
15. $7 + 5 = 12$
16. $9 + 5 = 14$
17. $8 + 7 = 15$
18. $9 + 3 = 12$
19. $8 + 2 = 10$
20. $9 + 4 = 13$
21. $8 + 8 = 16$
22. $11 + 3 = 14$
23. $8 + 3 = 11$
24. $9 + 8 = 17$
25. $6 + 6 = 12$
26. $7 + 3 = 10$
27. $9 + 9 = 18$

30 CD-104318 • © Carson-Dellosa

Page 31 — Sums to 18

Name _____ Date _____

Sums to 18

Total Problems: 27
Problems Correct: _____

Solve each problem.

You're a Math Superstar!

1. $7 + 5 = 12$
2. $5 + 9 = 14$
3. $8 + 4 = 12$
4. $5 + 3 = 8$
5. $9 + 5 = 14$
6. $8 + 8 = 16$
7. $3 + 7 = 10$
8. $10 + 3 = 13$
9. $11 + 7 = 18$
10. $9 + 2 = 11$
11. $6 + 4 = 10$
12. $6 + 7 = 13$
13. $7 + 8 = 15$
14. $9 + 3 = 12$
15. $2 + 9 = 11$
16. $7 + 9 = 16$
17. $7 + 2 = 9$
18. $3 + 8 = 11$
19. $4 + 6 = 10$
20. $11 + 2 = 13$
21. $2 + 4 = 6$
22. $3 + 2 = 5$
23. $8 + 9 = 17$
24. $4 + 0 = 4$
25. $4 + 9 = 13$
26. $16 + 0 = 16$
27. $4 + 7 = 11$

CD-104318 • © Carson-Dellosa 31

Sheet 1 (page 32)

Name _____ Date _____

Sums from 10 to 18

Total Problems: 27
Problems Correct: _____

Solve each problem.

Slide into Addition!

1. $7 + 6 = 13$
2. $2 + 9 = 11$
3. $4 + 8 = 12$
4. $6 + 5 = 11$
5. $9 + 7 = 16$
6. $9 + 9 = 18$
7. $6 + 8 = 14$
8. $5 + 9 = 14$
9. $8 + 9 = 17$
10. $3 + 9 = 12$
11. $7 + 9 = 16$
12. $9 + 8 = 17$
13. $8 + 7 = 15$
14. $6 + 9 = 15$
15. $8 + 6 = 14$
16. $9 + 5 = 14$
17. $10 + 3 = 13$
18. $7 + 7 = 14$
19. $4 + 9 = 13$
20. $5 + 8 = 13$
21. $16 + 2 = 18$
22. $8 + 8 = 16$
23. $6 + 4 = 10$
24. $7 + 3 = 10$
25. $9 + 6 = 15$
26. $5 + 7 = 12$
27. $7 + 8 = 15$

CD-104318 • © Carson-Dellosa

32

Sheet 2 (page 33)

Name _____ Date _____

Sums from 10 to 18

Total Problems: 27
Problems Correct: _____

Solve each problem.

Way to Go!

1. $8 + 9 = 17$
2. $8 + 3 = 11$
3. $7 + 9 = 16$
4. $6 + 8 = 14$
5. $7 + 6 = 13$
6. $9 + 6 = 15$
7. $6 + 9 = 15$
8. $7 + 8 = 15$
9. $11 + 0 = 11$
10. $3 + 9 = 12$
11. $8 + 4 = 12$
12. $9 + 7 = 16$
13. $7 + 7 = 14$
14. $5 + 9 = 14$
15. $8 + 6 = 14$
16. $14 + 1 = 15$
17. $9 + 4 = 13$
18. $6 + 7 = 13$
19. $2 + 8 = 10$
20. $9 + 8 = 17$
21. $6 + 6 = 12$
22. $8 + 7 = 15$
23. $7 + 5 = 12$
24. $5 + 5 = 10$
25. $9 + 9 = 18$
26. $6 + 4 = 10$
27. $10 + 2 = 12$

1st PLACE

CD-104318 • © Carson-Dellosa

33

Sheet 3 (page 34)

Name _____ Date _____

Sums from 10 to 18

Total Problems: 27
Problems Correct: _____

Solve each problem.

Addition Is Your Friend!

1. $6 + 7 = 13$
2. $8 + 9 = 17$
3. $8 + 8 = 16$
4. $9 + 6 = 15$
5. $7 + 9 = 16$
6. $9 + 9 = 18$
7. $8 + 7 = 15$
8. $6 + 5 = 11$
9. $7 + 8 = 15$
10. $9 + 5 = 14$
11. $9 + 2 = 11$
12. $4 + 8 = 12$
13. $5 + 7 = 12$
14. $7 + 3 = 10$
15. $10 + 8 = 18$
16. $8 + 6 = 14$
17. $11 + 3 = 14$
18. $8 + 5 = 13$
19. $8 + 3 = 11$
20. $8 + 2 = 10$
21. $7 + 7 = 14$
22. $5 + 6 = 11$
23. $2 + 12 = 14$
24. $5 + 8 = 13$
25. $9 + 7 = 16$
26. $5 + 5 = 10$
27. $9 + 8 = 17$

CD-104318 • © Carson-Dellosa

34

Sheet 4 (page 35)

Name _____ Date _____

Differences from 10 or Less

Total Problems: 27
Problems Correct: _____

Solve each problem.

A Good Attitude Is Key!

1. $9 - 6 = 3$
2. $8 - 2 = 6$
3. $10 - 0 = 10$
4. $10 - 9 = 1$
5. $10 - 3 = 7$
6. $9 - 6 = 3$
7. $4 - 2 = 2$
8. $7 - 4 = 3$
9. $10 - 4 = 6$
10. $10 - 10 = 0$
11. $9 - 4 = 5$
12. $10 - 2 = 8$
13. $8 - 6 = 2$
14. $10 - 5 = 5$
15. $7 - 5 = 2$
16. $9 - 5 = 4$
17. $8 - 5 = 3$
18. $8 - 7 = 1$
19. $7 - 3 = 4$
20. $3 - 2 = 1$
21. $10 - 3 = 7$
22. $6 - 2 = 4$
23. $10 - 1 = 9$
24. $9 - 3 = 6$
25. $7 - 6 = 1$
26. $10 - 4 = 6$
27. $10 - 8 = 2$

CD-104318 • © Carson-Dellosa

35

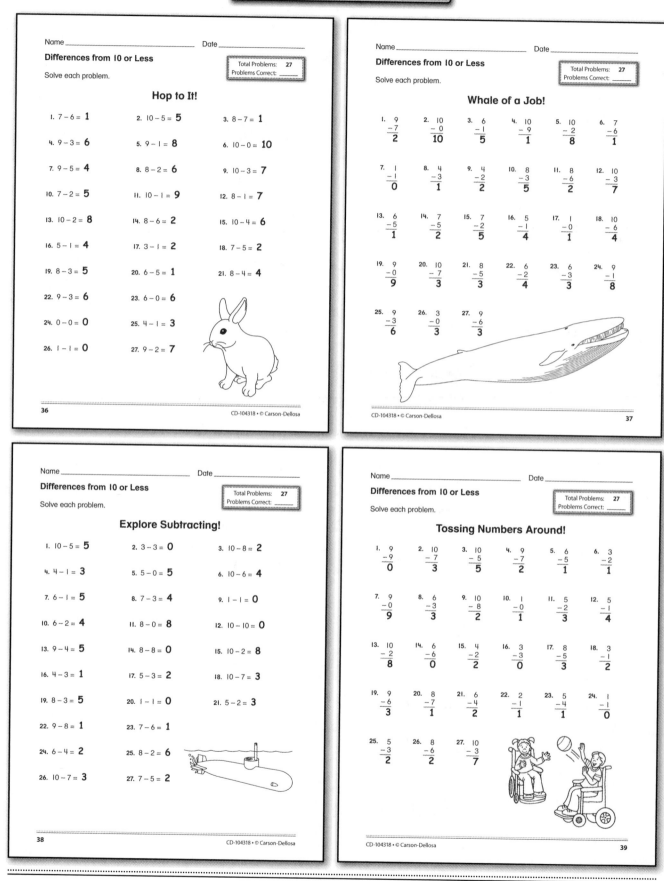

Name _____ Date _____

Differences from 10 or Less

Solve each problem.

Total Problems: 27
Problems Correct: _____

Hop to It!

1. 7 – 6 = **1**
2. 10 – 5 = **5**
3. 8 – 7 = **1**
4. 9 – 3 = **6**
5. 9 – 1 = **8**
6. 10 – 0 = **10**
7. 9 – 5 = **4**
8. 8 – 2 = **6**
9. 10 – 3 = **7**
10. 7 – 2 = **5**
11. 10 – 1 = **9**
12. 8 – 1 = **7**
13. 10 – 2 = **8**
14. 8 – 6 = **2**
15. 10 – 4 = **6**
16. 5 – 1 = **4**
17. 3 – 1 = **2**
18. 7 – 5 = **2**
19. 8 – 3 = **5**
20. 6 – 5 = **1**
21. 8 – 4 = **4**
22. 9 – 3 = **6**
23. 6 – 0 = **6**
24. 0 – 0 = **0**
25. 4 – 1 = **3**
26. 1 – 1 = **0**
27. 9 – 2 = **7**

36 • CD-104318 • © Carson-Dellosa

Name _____ Date _____

Differences from 10 or Less

Solve each problem.

Total Problems: 27
Problems Correct: _____

Whale of a Job!

1. 9 – 7 = **2**
2. 10 – 0 = **10**
3. 6 – 1 = **5**
4. 10 – 9 = **1**
5. 10 – 2 = **8**
6. 7 – 6 = **1**
7. 1 – 1 = **0**
8. 4 – 3 = **1**
9. 4 – 2 = **2**
10. 8 – 3 = **5**
11. 8 – 6 = **2**
12. 10 – 3 = **7**
13. 6 – 5 = **1**
14. 7 – 5 = **2**
15. 7 – 2 = **5**
16. 5 – 1 = **4**
17. 1 – 0 = **1**
18. 10 – 6 = **4**
19. 9 – 0 = **9**
20. 10 – 7 = **3**
21. 8 – 5 = **3**
22. 6 – 2 = **4**
23. 6 – 3 = **3**
24. 9 – 1 = **8**
25. 9 – 3 = **6**
26. 3 – 0 = **3**
27. 9 – 6 = **3**

CD-104318 • © Carson-Dellosa • 37

Name _____ Date _____

Differences from 10 or Less

Solve each problem.

Total Problems: 27
Problems Correct: _____

Explore Subtracting!

1. 10 – 5 = **5**
2. 3 – 3 = **0**
3. 10 – 8 = **2**
4. 4 – 1 = **3**
5. 5 – 0 = **5**
6. 10 – 6 = **4**
7. 6 – 1 = **5**
8. 7 – 3 = **4**
9. 1 – 1 = **0**
10. 6 – 2 = **4**
11. 8 – 0 = **8**
12. 10 – 10 = **0**
13. 9 – 4 = **5**
14. 8 – 8 = **0**
15. 10 – 2 = **8**
16. 4 – 3 = **1**
17. 5 – 3 = **2**
18. 10 – 7 = **3**
19. 8 – 3 = **5**
20. 1 – 1 = **0**
21. 5 – 2 = **3**
22. 9 – 8 = **1**
23. 7 – 6 = **1**
24. 6 – 4 = **2**
25. 8 – 2 = **6**
26. 10 – 7 = **3**
27. 7 – 5 = **2**

38 • CD-104318 • © Carson-Dellosa

Name _____ Date _____

Differences from 10 or Less

Solve each problem.

Total Problems: 27
Problems Correct: _____

Tossing Numbers Around!

1. 9 – 9 = **0**
2. 10 – 7 = **3**
3. 10 – 5 = **5**
4. 9 – 7 = **2**
5. 6 – 5 = **1**
6. 3 – 2 = **1**
7. 9 – 0 = **9**
8. 6 – 3 = **3**
9. 10 – 8 = **2**
10. 1 – 0 = **1**
11. 5 – 2 = **3**
12. 5 – 1 = **4**
13. 10 – 2 = **8**
14. 6 – 6 = **0**
15. 4 – 2 = **2**
16. 3 – 3 = **0**
17. 8 – 5 = **3**
18. 3 – 1 = **2**
19. 9 – 6 = **3**
20. 8 – 7 = **1**
21. 6 – 4 = **2**
22. 2 – 1 = **1**
23. 5 – 4 = **1**
24. 1 – 1 = **0**
25. 5 – 3 = **2**
26. 8 – 6 = **2**
27. 10 – 3 = **7**

CD-104318 • © Carson-Dellosa • 39

Worksheet 1 (page 40)

Name _____ Date _____

Differences from 11 or Less

Total Problems:	27
Problems Correct:	_____

Solve each problem.

Ace Subtraction!

1. $9 - 0 = $ **9**
2. $7 - 6 = $ **1**
3. $9 - 8 = $ **1**
4. $9 - 2 = $ **7**
5. $11 - 5 = $ **6**
6. $11 - 4 = $ **7**
7. $11 - 3 = $ **8**
8. $11 - 5 = $ **6**
9. $8 - 5 = $ **3**
10. $10 - 2 = $ **8**
11. $9 - 8 = $ **1**
12. $11 - 4 = $ **7**
13. $8 - 7 = $ **1**
14. $10 - 4 = $ **6**
15. $11 - 1 = $ **10**
16. $11 - 8 = $ **3**
17. $10 - 8 = $ **2**
18. $10 - 6 = $ **4**
19. $11 - 2 = $ **9**
20. $11 - 6 = $ **5**
21. $9 - 3 = $ **6**
22. $11 - 10 = $ **1**
23. $9 - 3 = $ **6**
24. $11 - 3 = $ **8**
25. $8 - 6 = $ **2**
26. $10 - 5 = $ **5**
27. $9 - 1 = $ **8**

40   CD-104318 • © Carson-Dellosa

Worksheet 2 (page 41)

Name _____ Date _____

Differences from 11 or Less

Total Problems:	27
Problems Correct:	_____

Solve each problem.

Slow and Steady!

1. $9 - 0 = $ **9**
2. $11 - 9 = $ **2**
3. $11 - 1 = $ **10**
4. $11 - 3 = $ **8**
5. $7 - 5 = $ **2**
6. $9 - 6 = $ **3**
7. $8 - 6 = $ **2**
8. $7 - 2 = $ **5**
9. $11 - 4 = $ **7**
10. $10 - 8 = $ **2**
11. $11 - 3 = $ **8**
12. $8 - 7 = $ **1**
13. $11 - 7 = $ **4**
14. $10 - 6 = $ **4**
15. $11 - 10 = $ **1**
16. $9 - 8 = $ **1**
17. $11 - 5 = $ **6**
18. $9 - 5 = $ **4**
19. $8 - 5 = $ **3**
20. $9 - 2 = $ **7**
21. $10 - 7 = $ **3**
22. $5 - 2 = $ **3**
23. $11 - 5 = $ **6**
24. $11 - 2 = $ **9**
25. $10 - 5 = $ **5**
26. $11 - 6 = $ **5**
27. $8 - 8 = $ **0**

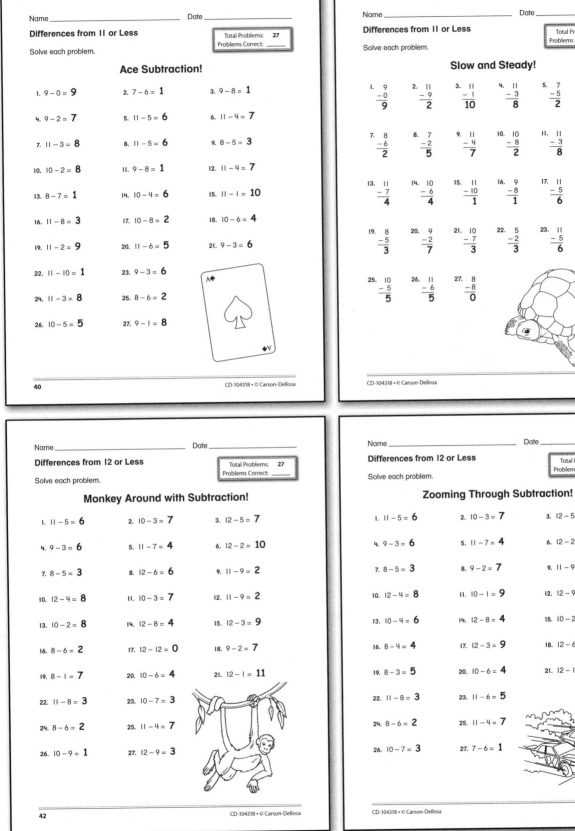

41   CD-104318 • © Carson-Dellosa

Worksheet 3 (page 42)

Name _____ Date _____

Differences from 12 or Less

Total Problems:	27
Problems Correct:	_____

Solve each problem.

Monkey Around with Subtraction!

1. $11 - 5 = $ **6**
2. $10 - 3 = $ **7**
3. $12 - 5 = $ **7**
4. $9 - 3 = $ **6**
5. $11 - 7 = $ **4**
6. $12 - 2 = $ **10**
7. $8 - 5 = $ **3**
8. $12 - 6 = $ **6**
9. $11 - 9 = $ **2**
10. $12 - 4 = $ **8**
11. $10 - 3 = $ **7**
12. $11 - 9 = $ **2**
13. $10 - 2 = $ **8**
14. $12 - 8 = $ **4**
15. $12 - 3 = $ **9**
16. $8 - 6 = $ **2**
17. $12 - 12 = $ **0**
18. $9 - 2 = $ **7**
19. $8 - 1 = $ **7**
20. $10 - 6 = $ **4**
21. $12 - 1 = $ **11**
22. $11 - 8 = $ **3**
23. $10 - 7 = $ **3**
24. $8 - 6 = $ **2**
25. $11 - 4 = $ **7**
26. $10 - 9 = $ **1**
27. $12 - 9 = $ **3**

42   CD-104318 • © Carson-Dellosa

Worksheet 4 (page 43)

Name _____ Date _____

Differences from 12 or Less

Total Problems:	27
Problems Correct:	_____

Solve each problem.

Zooming Through Subtraction!

1. $11 - 5 = $ **6**
2. $10 - 3 = $ **7**
3. $12 - 5 = $ **7**
4. $9 - 3 = $ **6**
5. $11 - 7 = $ **4**
6. $12 - 2 = $ **10**
7. $8 - 5 = $ **3**
8. $9 - 2 = $ **7**
9. $11 - 9 = $ **2**
10. $12 - 4 = $ **8**
11. $10 - 1 = $ **9**
12. $12 - 9 = $ **3**
13. $10 - 4 = $ **6**
14. $12 - 8 = $ **4**
15. $10 - 2 = $ **8**
16. $8 - 4 = $ **4**
17. $12 - 3 = $ **9**
18. $12 - 6 = $ **6**
19. $8 - 3 = $ **5**
20. $10 - 6 = $ **4**
21. $12 - 1 = $ **11**
22. $11 - 8 = $ **3**
23. $11 - 6 = $ **5**
24. $8 - 6 = $ **2**
25. $11 - 4 = $ **7**
26. $10 - 7 = $ **3**
27. $7 - 6 = $ **1**

43   CD-104318 • © Carson-Dellosa

Name _____ **Date** _____

Differences from 13 or Less

Solve each problem.

Total Problems: 27
Problems Correct: _____

You're on the Right Track!

1. 11 − 5 = **6**	2. 12 − 4 = **8**	3. 10 − 5 = **5**	4. 13 − 4 = **9**	5. 10 − 9 = **1**	6. 12 − 4 = **8**
7. 13 − 5 = **8**	8. 10 − 6 = **4**	9. 12 − 6 = **6**	10. 12 − 3 = **9**	11. 13 − 7 = **6**	12. 12 − 5 = **7**
13. 13 − 8 = **5**	14. 13 − 9 = **4**	15. 12 − 4 = **8**	16. 11 − 6 = **5**	17. 10 − 4 = **6**	18. 11 − 8 = **3**
19. 13 − 5 = **8**	20. 12 − 7 = **5**	21. 13 − 7 = **6**	22. 10 − 3 = **7**	23. 12 − 6 = **6**	24. 12 − 8 = **4**
25. 12 − 9 = **3**	26. 11 − 7 = **4**	27. 10 − 8 = **2**			

44 CD-104318 • © Carson-Dellosa

Name _____ **Date** _____

Differences from 14 or Less

Solve each problem.

Total Problems: 27
Problems Correct: _____

Have a Ball Subtracting!

1. 12 − 5 = **7**	2. 13 − 7 = **6**	3. 12 − 8 = **4**	4. 13 − 6 = **7**	5. 13 − 8 = **5**	6. 10 − 8 = **2**
7. 14 − 8 = **6**	8. 10 − 4 = **6**	9. 14 − 6 = **8**	10. 13 − 4 = **9**	11. 12 − 7 = **5**	12. 11 − 9 = **2**
13. 13 − 9 = **4**	14. 14 − 4 = **10**	15. 14 − 9 = **5**	16. 12 − 6 = **6**	17. 13 − 9 = **4**	18. 14 − 2 = **12**
19. 14 − 7 = **7**	20. 14 − 5 = **9**	21. 10 − 6 = **4**	22. 14 − 2 = **12**	23. 11 − 8 = **3**	24. 12 − 9 = **3**
25. 13 − 5 = **8**	26. 11 − 2 = **9**	27. 11 − 0 = **11**			

CD-104318 • © Carson-Dellosa 45

Name _____ **Date** _____

Differences from 14 or Less

Solve each problem.

Total Problems: 27
Problems Correct: _____

Be a Fan of Subtraction!

1. 11 − 8 = **3**	2. 7 − 2 = **5**	3. 14 − 8 = **6**	4. 13 − 6 = **7**	5. 8 − 3 = **5**	6. 10 − 6 = **4**
7. 13 − 9 = **4**	8. 12 − 8 = **4**	9. 10 − 9 = **1**	10. 10 − 7 = **3**	11. 11 − 4 = **7**	12. 14 − 6 = **8**
13. 12 − 6 = **6**	14. 13 − 7 = **6**	15. 12 − 9 = **3**	16. 11 − 3 = **8**	17. 13 − 4 = **9**	18. 11 − 7 = **4**
19. 11 − 5 = **6**	20. 10 − 2 = **8**	21. 14 − 5 = **9**	22. 12 − 4 = **8**	23. 12 − 5 = **7**	24. 13 − 5 = **8**
25. 11 − 7 = **4**	26. 12 − 3 = **9**	27. 14 − 9 = **5**			

46 CD-104318 • © Carson-Dellosa

Name _____ **Date** _____

Differences from 14 or Less

Solve each problem.

Total Problems: 27
Problems Correct: _____

Get Jazzed About Subtraction!

1. 11 − 2 = **9**	2. 10 − 5 = **5**	3. 11 − 3 = **8**	4. 10 − 3 = **7**	5. 11 − 6 = **5**	6. 12 − 9 = **3**
7. 10 − 4 = **6**	8. 6 − 3 = **3**	9. 14 − 8 = **6**	10. 12 − 3 = **9**	11. 12 − 6 = **6**	12. 11 − 4 = **7**
13. 8 − 4 = **4**	14. 12 − 5 = **7**	15. 13 − 4 = **9**	16. 11 − 5 = **6**	17. 13 − 8 = **5**	18. 14 − 5 = **9**
19. 12 − 8 = **4**	20. 14 − 9 = **5**	21. 12 − 5 = **8**	22. 12 − 4 = **8**	23. 13 − 6 = **7**	24. 9 − 6 = **3**
25. 13 − 9 = **4**	26. 12 − 7 = **5**	27. 14 − 7 = **7**			

CD-104318 • © Carson-Dellosa 47

Worksheet 1 (page 48)

Differences from 14 or Less

Solve each problem.

Total Problems: 27
Problems Correct: _____

You Can Do It!

1. 13 − 6 = 7	2. 10 − 8 = 2	3. 12 − 8 = 4	4. 13 − 4 = 9	5. 12 − 4 = 8	6. 13 − 7 = 6
7. 11 − 7 = 4	8. 14 − 7 = 7	9. 12 − 3 = 9	10. 9 − 7 = 2	11. 6 − 2 = 4	12. 11 − 6 = 5
13. 5 − 3 = 2	14. 11 − 8 = 3	15. 12 − 6 = 6	16. 10 − 1 = 9	17. 12 − 5 = 7	18. 12 − 7 = 5
19. 13 − 5 = 8	20. 13 − 9 = 4	21. 11 − 2 = 9	22. 13 − 8 = 5	23. 11 − 3 = 8	24. 8 − 5 = 3
25. 14 − 8 = 6	26. 11 − 9 = 2	27. 7 − 4 = 3			

Worksheet 2 (page 49)

Differences from 15 or Less

Solve each problem.

Total Problems: 27
Problems Correct: _____

Great Job!

1. 10 − 9 = 1	2. 15 − 9 = 6	3. 13 − 5 = 8	4. 15 − 8 = 7	5. 12 − 7 = 5	6. 14 − 6 = 8
7. 10 − 4 = 6	8. 12 − 8 = 4	9. 13 − 9 = 4	10. 15 − 5 = 10	11. 12 − 5 = 7	12. 15 − 3 = 12
13. 14 − 5 = 9	14. 12 − 6 = 6	15. 12 − 4 = 8	16. 11 − 6 = 5	17. 15 − 2 = 13	18. 10 − 6 = 4
19. 13 − 6 = 7	20. 13 − 8 = 5	21. 12 − 9 = 3	22. 13 − 3 = 10	23. 15 − 7 = 8	24. 14 − 7 = 7
25. 15 − 8 = 7	26. 10 − 5 = 5	27. 15 − 1 = 14			

Worksheet 3 (page 50)

Differences from 10 to 18

Solve each problem.

Total Problems: 27
Problems Correct: _____

Pace Yourself!

1. 13 − 8 = 5	2. 15 − 6 = 9	3. 17 − 8 = 9	4. 16 − 9 = 7	5. 18 − 9 = 9	6. 14 − 9 = 5
7. 13 − 9 = 4	8. 13 − 6 = 7	9. 12 − 6 = 6	10. 10 − 3 = 7	11. 12 − 9 = 3	12. 15 − 9 = 6
13. 15 − 8 = 7	14. 11 − 9 = 2	15. 15 − 7 = 8	16. 11 − 8 = 3	17. 16 − 7 = 9	18. 10 − 4 = 6
19. 14 − 5 = 9	20. 12 − 7 = 5	21. 17 − 9 = 8	22. 10 − 3 = 7	23. 16 − 8 = 8	24. 16 − 9 = 7
25. 12 − 3 = 9	26. 14 − 6 = 8	27. 11 − 7 = 4			

Worksheet 4 (page 51)

Differences from 10 to 18

Solve each problem.

Total Problems: 27
Problems Correct: _____

Now You're Singing!

1. 10 − 5 = 5	2. 15 − 6 = 9	3. 12 − 8 = 4	4. 12 − 6 = 6	5. 13 − 7 = 6	6. 12 − 5 = 7
7. 17 − 9 = 8	8. 11 − 8 = 3	9. 11 − 9 = 2	10. 18 − 9 = 9	11. 14 − 5 = 9	12. 14 − 9 = 5
13. 14 − 6 = 8	14. 13 − 9 = 4	15. 14 − 8 = 6	16. 11 − 3 = 8	17. 16 − 8 = 8	18. 15 − 8 = 7
19. 10 − 2 = 8	20. 16 − 7 = 9	21. 15 − 9 = 6	22. 11 − 2 = 9	23. 16 − 9 = 7	24. 15 − 7 = 8
25. 13 − 4 = 9	26. 13 − 8 = 5	27. 10 − 8 = 2			

Page 52

Name _____ Date _____

Differences from 10 to 18

Solve each problem.

Total Problems: **27**
Problems Correct: _____

You're a Winner!

1. $18 - 9 = $ **9**
2. $10 - 5 = $ **5**
3. $13 - 7 = $ **6**
4. $14 - 6 = $ **8**
5. $15 - 6 = $ **9**
6. $12 - 3 = $ **9**
7. $15 - 7 = $ **8**
8. $14 - 9 = $ **5**
9. $17 - 8 = $ **9**
10. $11 - 7 = $ **4**
11. $13 - 4 = $ **9**
12. $11 - 4 = $ **7**
13. $12 - 6 = $ **6**
14. $15 - 9 = $ **6**
15. $11 - 5 = $ **6**
16. $10 - 1 = $ **9**
17. $14 - 8 = $ **6**
18. $16 - 8 = $ **8**
19. $10 - 2 = $ **8**
20. $13 - 5 = $ **8**
21. $10 - 8 = $ **2**
22. $11 - 2 = $ **9**
23. $10 - 9 = $ **1**
24. $11 - 8 = $ **3**
25. $13 - 8 = $ **5**
26. $17 - 9 = $ **8**
27. $16 - 7 = $ **9**

52   CD-104318 • © Carson-Dellosa

Page 53

Name _____ Date _____

Addition and Subtraction Through 6

Solve each problem.

Total Problems: **27**
Problems Correct: _____

Build Your Math Skills!

1. $4 - 0 = $ **4**
2. $4 + 0 = $ **4**
3. $0 + 3 = $ **3**
4. $1 + 1 = $ **2**
5. $2 - 1 = $ **1**
6. $1 + 4 = $ **5**
7. $2 + 3 = $ **5**
8. $3 + 2 = $ **5**
9. $6 - 6 = $ **0**
10. $4 - 3 = $ **1**
11. $1 + 4 = $ **5**
12. $1 + 3 = $ **4**
13. $5 - 2 = $ **3**
14. $2 - 2 = $ **0**
15. $4 - 2 = $ **2**
16. $2 + 1 = $ **3**
17. $2 + 2 = $ **4**
18. $3 - 3 = $ **0**
19. $6 - 2 = $ **4**
20. $6 - 5 = $ **1**
21. $4 + 1 = $ **5**
22. $2 + 3 = $ **5**
23. $6 - 1 = $ **5**
24. $3 - 1 = $ **2**
25. $5 - 1 = $ **4**
26. $1 + 0 = $ **1**
27. $6 + 0 = $ **6**

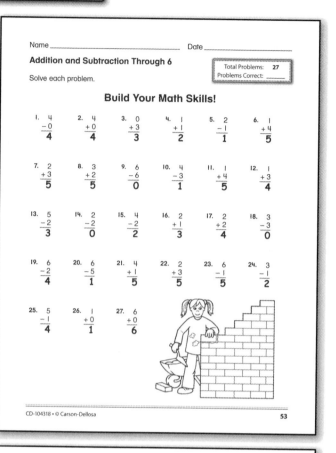

CD-104318 • © Carson-Dellosa   53

Page 54

Name _____ Date _____

Addition and Subtraction Through 6

Solve each problem.

Total Problems: **27**
Problems Correct: _____

One Bite at a Time!

1. $6 - 0 = $ **6**
2. $1 + 0 = $ **1**
3. $2 + 3 = $ **5**
4. $4 + 1 = $ **5**
5. $5 - 1 = $ **4**
6. $4 + 1 = $ **5**
7. $4 + 0 = $ **4**
8. $3 + 2 = $ **5**
9. $6 - 6 = $ **0**
10. $3 + 3 = $ **6**
11. $2 + 1 = $ **3**
12. $1 + 3 = $ **4**
13. $4 - 2 = $ **2**
14. $5 - 2 = $ **3**
15. $2 - 2 = $ **0**
16. $4 + 1 = $ **5**
17. $2 + 2 = $ **4**
18. $4 - 3 = $ **1**
19. $6 - 2 = $ **4**
20. $6 - 5 = $ **1**
21. $1 + 1 = $ **2**
22. $2 + 3 = $ **5**
23. $3 - 1 = $ **2**
24. $2 - 1 = $ **1**
25. $6 - 1 = $ **5**
26. $6 + 0 = $ **6**
27. $0 + 3 = $ **3**

54   CD-104318 • © Carson-Dellosa

Page 55

Name _____ Date _____

Addition and Subtraction Through 6

Solve each problem.

Total Problems: **27**
Problems Correct: _____

Whale of a Job!

1. $3 + 3 = $ **6**
2. $5 - 1 = $ **4**
3. $2 + 2 = $ **4**
4. $4 - 2 = $ **2**
5. $4 + 2 = $ **6**
6. $2 - 1 = $ **1**
7. $0 + 5 = $ **5**
8. $3 - 2 = $ **1**
9. $7 - 2 = $ **5**
10. $3 + 1 = $ **4**
11. $2 - 1 = $ **1**
12. $1 + 3 = $ **4**
13. $0 - 0 = $ **0**
14. $1 + 2 = $ **3**
15. $6 - 5 = $ **1**
16. $2 + 4 = $ **6**
17. $6 - 2 = $ **4**
18. $7 - 1 = $ **6**
19. $0 + 6 = $ **6**
20. $6 - 2 = $ **4**
21. $1 + 5 = $ **6**
22. $6 - 3 = $ **3**
23. $1 + 4 = $ **5**
24. $5 - 4 = $ **1**
25. $3 + 2 = $ **5**
26. $4 - 1 = $ **3**
27. $6 + 0 = $ **6**

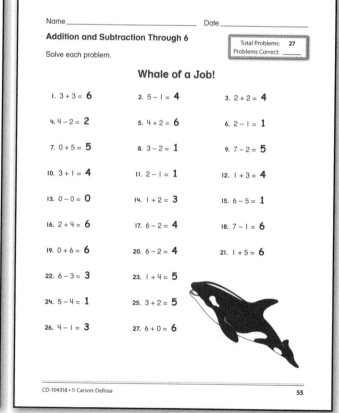

CD-104318 • © Carson-Dellosa   55

Worksheet 1 (page 56)

Name _____ Date _____

Addition and Subtraction Through 10

Total Problems: 27
Problems Correct: _____

Solve each problem.

Look at You Go!

1. $10 - 6 = 4$
2. $9 + 1 = 10$
3. $6 + 3 = 9$
4. $8 + 1 = 9$
5. $9 - 5 = 4$
6. $6 + 4 = 10$

7. $2 + 3 = 5$
8. $3 + 5 = 8$
9. $9 - 0 = 9$
10. $6 - 2 = 4$
11. $7 + 1 = 8$
12. $0 + 3 = 3$

13. $8 - 4 = 4$
14. $5 - 1 = 4$
15. $10 - 2 = 8$
16. $4 + 4 = 8$
17. $8 + 2 = 10$
18. $9 - 4 = 5$

19. $6 - 3 = 3$
20. $10 - 5 = 5$
21. $9 + 0 = 9$
22. $7 + 3 = 10$
23. $9 - 6 = 3$
24. $7 - 7 = 0$

25. $8 - 5 = 3$
26. $5 + 4 = 9$
27. $6 + 2 = 8$

56   CD-104318 • © Carson-Dellosa

Worksheet 2 (page 57)

Name _____ Date _____

Addition and Subtraction Through 10

Total Problems: 27
Problems Correct: _____

Solve each problem.

Who-oo Likes to Add and Subtract?

1. $8 - 5 = 3$
2. $5 + 5 = 10$
3. $2 + 7 = 9$
4. $7 + 3 = 10$
5. $9 - 6 = 3$
6. $5 + 4 = 9$

7. $6 + 3 = 9$
8. $2 + 6 = 8$
9. $10 - 4 = 6$
10. $8 + 2 = 10$
11. $5 + 1 = 6$
12. $6 - 3 = 3$

13. $9 - 4 = 5$
14. $8 - 7 = 1$
15. $9 + 1 = 10$
16. $3 + 4 = 7$
17. $8 - 2 = 6$
18. $10 - 10 = 0$

19. $9 - 3 = 6$
20. $2 + 3 = 5$
21. $5 + 3 = 8$
22. $5 - 4 = 1$
23. $8 - 4 = 4$
24. $7 - 4 = 3$

25. $6 + 4 = 10$
26. $6 + 2 = 8$
27. $5 + 3 = 8$

CD-104318 • © Carson-Dellosa   57

Worksheet 3 (page 58)

Name _____ Date _____

Addition and Subtraction Through 10

Total Problems: 27
Problems Correct: _____

Solve each problem.

Get Moving!

1. $6 + 3 = 9$
2. $8 - 6 = 2$
3. $5 + 3 = 8$
4. $10 - 0 = 10$
5. $9 + 0 = 9$
6. $9 - 1 = 8$
7. $8 + 1 = 9$
8. $6 + 3 = 9$
9. $7 - 2 = 5$
10. $5 + 1 = 6$
11. $9 - 2 = 7$
12. $5 + 4 = 9$
13. $6 - 4 = 2$
14. $7 + 3 = 10$
15. $8 - 2 = 6$
16. $2 + 6 = 8$
17. $10 - 6 = 4$
18. $10 - 1 = 9$
19. $6 + 4 = 10$
20. $8 - 2 = 6$
21. $2 + 7 = 9$
22. $8 - 5 = 3$
23. $5 + 5 = 10$
24. $10 - 10 = 0$
25. $3 + 4 = 7$
26. $9 - 3 = 6$
27. $9 + 1 = 10$

58   CD-104318 • © Carson-Dellosa

Worksheet 4 (page 59)

Name _____ Date _____

Addition and Subtraction Through 10

Total Problems: 27
Problems Correct: _____

Solve each problem.

Ready! Set! Add and Subtract!

1. $5 - 2 = 3$
2. $6 + 3 = 9$
3. $5 + 2 = 7$
4. $5 + 3 = 8$
5. $3 - 1 = 2$
6. $4 + 3 = 7$

7. $7 + 3 = 10$
8. $4 + 2 = 6$
9. $8 - 6 = 2$
10. $9 - 8 = 1$
11. $4 + 1 = 5$
12. $1 + 9 = 10$

13. $10 - 5 = 5$
14. $7 - 5 = 2$
15. $5 - 2 = 3$
16. $5 + 5 = 10$
17. $2 + 8 = 10$
18. $6 - 2 = 4$

19. $6 - 3 = 3$
20. $8 - 4 = 4$
21. $1 + 5 = 6$
22. $2 + 3 = 5$
23. $5 - 1 = 4$
24. $9 - 5 = 4$

25. $7 - 7 = 0$
26. $4 + 2 = 6$
27. $6 + 4 = 10$

CD-104318 • © Carson-Dellosa   59

Answer Key

Addition and Subtraction Through 11

Name _____ Date _____

Solve each problem.

Total Problems: 27
Problems Correct: _____

Math Is Smooth Sailing!

1. $10 - 7 = 3$	2. $7 + 3 = 10$	3. $9 + 1 = 10$	4. $6 + 5 = 11$	5. $10 - 3 = 7$	6. $6 + 4 = 10$
7. $7 + 3 = 10$	8. $5 + 6 = 11$	9. $11 - 4 = 7$	10. $11 - 9 = 2$	11. $5 + 4 = 9$	12. $4 + 7 = 11$
13. $11 - 2 = 9$	14. $10 - 4 = 6$	15. $9 - 2 = 7$	16. $7 + 3 = 10$	17. $9 + 2 = 11$	18. $10 - 8 = 2$
19. $11 - 7 = 4$	20. $10 - 5 = 5$	21. $10 + 1 = 11$	22. $8 + 3 = 11$	23. $11 - 6 = 5$	24. $10 - 6 = 4$
25. $8 - 1 = 7$	26. $8 + 2 = 10$	27. $5 + 5 = 10$			

60
CD-104318 • © Carson-Dellosa

Addition and Subtraction Through 12

Name _____ Date _____

Solve each problem.

Total Problems: 27
Problems Correct: _____

Mix It Up!

1. $10 - 7 = 3$	2. $3 + 8 = 11$	3. $6 + 6 = 12$	4. $6 + 3 = 9$	5. $11 - 5 = 6$	6. $12 - 2 = 10$
7. $6 + 5 = 11$	8. $8 + 4 = 12$	9. $10 - 4 = 6$	10. $11 - 3 = 8$	11. $9 + 2 = 11$	12. $7 + 3 = 10$
13. $11 - 4 = 7$	14. $11 - 2 = 9$	15. $12 - 4 = 8$	16. $6 + 5 = 11$	17. $5 + 2 = 7$	18. $12 - 5 = 7$
19. $12 - 3 = 9$	20. $11 - 6 = 5$	21. $8 + 2 = 10$	22. $9 + 3 = 12$	23. $11 - 8 = 3$	24. $12 - 6 = 6$
25. $10 - 1 = 9$	26. $7 + 5 = 12$	27. $5 + 5 = 10$			

CD-104318 • © Carson-Dellosa
61

Addition and Subtraction Through 14

Name _____ Date _____

Solve each problem.

Total Problems: 27
Problems Correct: _____

Spread Your Math Wings!

1. $12 - 7 = 5$	2. $9 + 0 = 9$	3. $5 + 7 = 12$	4. $8 + 5 = 13$	5. $14 - 8 = 6$	6. $6 + 4 = 10$
7. $5 + 9 = 14$	8. $6 + 7 = 13$	9. $11 - 6 = 5$	10. $13 - 8 = 5$	11. $6 + 8 = 14$	12. $7 + 7 = 14$
13. $12 - 5 = 7$	14. $10 - 2 = 8$	15. $11 - 8 = 3$	16. $8 + 5 = 13$	17. $2 + 9 = 11$	18. $12 - 6 = 6$
19. $12 - 3 = 9$	20. $13 - 7 = 6$	21. $5 + 6 = 11$	22. $3 + 9 = 12$	23. $13 - 4 = 9$	24. $10 - 1 = 9$
25. $14 - 7 = 7$	26. $4 + 8 = 12$	27. $8 + 4 = 12$			

62
CD-104318 • © Carson-Dellosa

Addition and Subtraction Through 18

Name _____ Date _____

Solve each problem.

Total Problems: 27
Problems Correct: _____

Relax with Math!

1. $15 - 6 = 9$	2. $9 + 9 = 18$	3. $6 + 9 = 15$	4. $12 + 1 = 13$	5. $12 - 9 = 3$	6. $8 + 9 = 17$
7. $6 + 7 = 13$	8. $10 + 2 = 12$	9. $13 - 6 = 7$	10. $15 - 7 = 8$	11. $8 + 8 = 16$	12. $8 + 3 = 11$
13. $16 - 8 = 8$	14. $15 - 8 = 7$	15. $11 - 2 = 9$	16. $9 + 2 = 11$	17. $14 + 2 = 16$	18. $18 - 9 = 9$
19. $14 - 6 = 8$	20. $15 - 5 = 10$	21. $4 + 9 = 13$	22. $7 + 8 = 15$	23. $16 - 7 = 9$	24. $17 - 9 = 8$
25. $15 - 9 = 6$	26. $11 + 5 = 16$	27. $16 + 0 = 16$			

CD-104318 • © Carson-Dellosa
63

CD-104318 • © Carson-Dellosa

Name _____ **Date** _____

Missing Addends

Total Problems: **27**
Problems Correct: _____

Solve each problem.

Discover Missing Addends!

1. 6 +[2] = 8
2. 0 +[7] = 7
3. 1 +[6] = 7
4. 4 +[4] = 8
5. 8 +[1] = 9
6. 1 +[1] = 2
7. 2 +[7] = 9
8. 3 +[7] = 10
9. 2 +[3] = 5
10. 4 +[1] = 5
11. 4 +[6] = 10
12. 6 +[3] = 9
13. 1 +[5] = 6
14. 3 +[6] = 9
15. 8 +[2] = 10
16. 7 +[0] = 7
17. 2 +[5] = 7
18. 5 +[4] = 9
19. 6 +[4] = 10
20. 6 +[2] = 8
21. 2 +[8] = 10
22. 3 +[2] = 5
23. 3 +[4] = 7
24. 4 +[4] = 8
25. 2 +[3] = 5
26. 5 +[4] = 9
27. 7 +[2] = 9

 CD-104318 • © Carson-Dellosa

Name _____ **Date** _____

Missing Addends

Total Problems: **27**
Problems Correct: _____

Solve each problem.

Finding Missing Addends Is a Breeze!

1. 8 +[4] = 12
2. 5 +[9] = 14
3. 9 +[9] = 18
4. 4 +[9] = 13
5. 8 +[9] = 17
6. 7 +[4] = 11
7. 6 +[8] = 14
8. 8 +[8] = 16
9. 3 +[8] = 11
10. 9 +[4] = 13
11. 9 +[6] = 15
12. 10 +[2] = 12
13. 6 +[7] = 13
14. 7 +[9] = 16
15. 7 +[5] = 12
16. 6 +[5] = 11
17. 5 +[5] = 10
18. 6 +[6] = 12
19. 8 +[6] = 14
20. 9 +[5] = 14
21. 8 +[8] = 16
22. 9 +[2] = 11
23. 7 +[7] = 14
24. 6 +[9] = 15
25. 8 +[5] = 13
26. 7 +[8] = 15
27. 4 +[9] = 13

CD-104318 • © Carson-Dellosa

Name _____ **Date** _____

Missing Addends

Total Problems: **27**
Problems Correct: _____

Solve each problem.

Find the Missing Pieces!

1. 9 +[4] = 13
2. 6 +[7] = 13
3. 9 +[9] = 18
4. 4 +[9] = 13
5. 4 +[6] = 10
6. 7 +[9] = 16
7. 7 +[4] = 11
8. 6 +[8] = 14
9. 8 +[6] = 14
10. 8 +[4] = 12
11. 5 +[6] = 11
12. 9 +[4] = 13
13. 9 +[6] = 15
14. 10 +[2] = 12
15. 10 +[8] = 18
16. 8 +[8] = 16
17. 7 +[5] = 12
18. 6 +[5] = 11
19. 5 +[5] = 10
20. 7 +[3] = 10
21. 8 +[7] = 15
22. 5 +[8] = 13
23. 14 +[2] = 16
24. 9 +[6] = 15
25. 5 +[11] = 16
26. 6 +[6] = 12
27. 8 +[6] = 14

 CD-104318 • © Carson-Dellosa

Name _____ **Date** _____

Addition with Three Addends

Total Problems: **27**
Problems Correct: _____

Solve each problem.

Build Your Addition Skills!

1. 1, 1, +4 = 6
2. 5, 0, +1 = 6
3. 2, 2, +2 = 6
4. 1, 1, +1 = 3
5. 6, 0, +0 = 6
6. 3, 0, +2 = 5
7. 1, 2, +3 = 6
8. 2, 4, +0 = 6
9. 1, 2, +2 = 5
10. 4, 1, +0 = 5
11. 3, 0, +2 = 5
12. 3, 1, +1 = 5
13. 0, 3, +1 = 4
14. 3, 1, +1 = 5
15. 3, 0, +3 = 6
16. 2, 1, +1 = 4
17. 1, 0, +5 = 6
18. 5, 1, +0 = 6
19. 2, 4, +0 = 6
20. 4, 2, +0 = 6
21. 3, 0, +0 = 3
22. 2, 2, +1 = 5
23. 2, 2, +2 = 6
24. 1, 1, +3 = 5
25. 5, 0, +0 = 5
26. 2, 1, +3 = 6
27. 0, 0, +0 = 0

CD-104318 • © Carson-Dellosa

Name _____ Date _____

Addition with Three Addends

Solve each problem.

Total Problems: 27
Problems Correct: _____

Addition Is a Breeze!

1. 3 + 1 + 1 = **5**
2. 4 + 1 + 1 = **6**
3. 1 + 0 + 1 = **2**
4. 1 + 2 + 2 = **5**
5. 4 + 6 + 7 = **17**
6. 2 + 2 + 2 = **6**
7. 4 + 6 + 3 = **13**
8. 1 + 2 + 3 = **6**
9. 4 + 0 + 2 = **6**
10. 1 + 1 + 2 = **4**
11. 0 + 4 + 1 = **5**
12. 0 + 2 + 4 = **6**
13. 4 + 2 + 0 = **6**
14. 3 + 1 + 0 = **4**
15. 0 + 2 + 3 = **5**
16. 2 + 1 + 0 = **3**
17. 2 + 1 + 1 = **4**
18. 3 + 0 + 1 = **4**
19. 2 + 0 + 2 = **4**
20. 1 + 2 + 1 = **4**
21. 2 + 0 + 1 = **3**
22. 3 + 0 + 2 = **5**
23. 3 + 1 + 2 = **6**
24. 1 + 1 + 3 = **5**
25. 1 + 1 + 1 = **3**
26. 0 + 3 + 1 = **4**
27. 2 + 0 + 3 = **5**

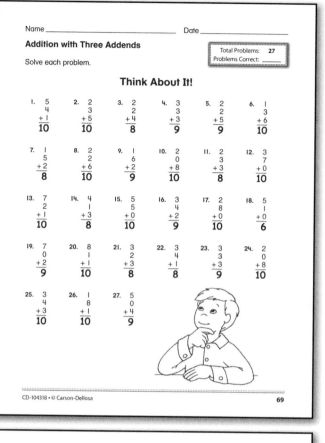

68   CD-104318 • © Carson-Dellosa

Name _____ Date _____

Addition with Three Addends

Solve each problem.

Total Problems: 27
Problems Correct: _____

Think About It!

1. 5
    4
  + 1

   10

2. 2
    3
  + 5

   10

3. 2
    2
  + 4

    8

4. 3
    3
  + 3

    9

5. 2
    2
  + 5

    9

6. 1
    3
  + 6

   10

7. 1
    5
  + 2

    8

8. 2
    2
  + 6

   10

9. 1
    6
  + 2

    9

10. 2
     0
   + 8

    10

11. 2
     3
   + 3

     8

12. 3
     7
   + 0

    10

13. 7
     2
   + 1

    10

14. 4
     1
   + 3

     8

15. 5
     5
   + 0

    10

16. 3
     4
   + 2

     9

17. 2
     8
   + 0

    10

18. 5
     1
   + 0

     6

19. 7
     0
   + 2

     9

20. 8
     1
   + 1

    10

21. 3
     2
   + 3

     8

22. 3
     4
   + 1

     8

23. 3
     3
   + 3

     9

24. 2
     0
   + 8

    10

25. 3
     4
   + 3

    10

26. 1
     8
   + 1

    10

27. 5
     0
   + 4

     9

CD-104318 • © Carson-Dellosa   69

Name _____ Date _____

Addition with Three Addends

Solve each problem.

Total Problems: 27
Problems Correct: _____

Take a Close Look!

1. 2 + 0 + 3 = **5**
2. 5 + 3 + 1 = **9**
3. 6 + 2 + 0 = **8**
4. 6 + 3 + 1 = **10**
5. 6 + 0 + 1 = **7**
6. 4 + 0 + 2 = **6**
7. 3 + 0 + 4 = **7**
8. 3 + 3 + 3 = **9**
9. 2 + 2 + 6 = **10**
10. 7 + 0 + 1 = **8**
11. 2 + 3 + 2 = **7**
12. 8 + 0 + 1 = **9**
13. 5 + 1 + 1 = **7**
14. 3 + 6 + 1 = **10**
15. 2 + 2 + 2 = **6**
16. 7 + 2 + 1 = **10**
17. 5 + 2 + 3 = **10**
18. 6 + 1 + 0 = **7**
19. 2 + 4 + 1 = **7**
20. 5 + 1 + 3 = **9**
21. 4 + 2 + 3 = **9**
22. 3 + 0 + 3 = **6**
23. 3 + 3 + 2 = **8**
24. 6 + 2 + 0 = **8**
25. 6 + 1 + 2 = **9**
26. 5 + 4 + 1 = **10**
27. 6 + 3 + 1 = **10**

70   CD-104318 • © Carson-Dellosa

Name _____ Date _____

Addition with Three Addends

Solve each problem.

Total Problems: 27
Problems Correct: _____

One Bite at a Time!

1. 9
    0
  + 4

   13

2. 10
     0
   + 5

    15

3. 2
    3
  + 6

   11

4. 3
    4
  + 7

   14

5. 2
    8
  + 5

   15

6. 6
    0
  + 5

   11

7. 12
     5
   + 6

    23

8. 2
    9
  + 2

   13

9. 4
    1
  + 9

   14

10. 2
     3
   + 6

    11

11. 8
     1
   + 7

    16

12. 5
     2
   + 6

    13

13. 11
     7
   + 1

    19

14. 11
     7
   + 6

    24

15. 6
     2
   + 4

    12

16. 7
     0
   + 7

    14

17. 4
     1
   + 6

    11

18. 3
     9
   + 4

    16

19. 1
     5
   + 6

    12

20. 1
     7
   + 6

    14

21. 5
     4
   + 7

    16

22. 3
     2
   + 9

    14

23. 12
     0
   + 6

    18

24. 6
     6
   + 2

    14

25. 3
     6
   + 9

    18

26. 2
     4
   + 5

    11

27. 9
     8
   + 0

    17

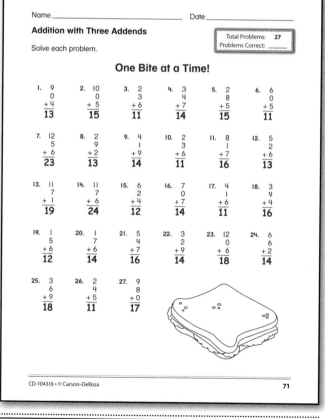

CD-104318 • © Carson-Dellosa   71

Name _____ Date _____

Addition with Three Addends

Total Problems: **27**
Problems Correct: _____

Solve each problem.

Keep Up the Good Work!

1. 5 3 + 4 = **12**	2. 10 0 + 5 = **15**	3. 7 2 + 8 = **17**	4. 4 5 + 2 = **11**	5. 2 3 + 9 = **14**	6. 8 7 + 2 = **17**
7. 4 5 + 7 = **16**	8. 6 2 + 6 = **14**	9. 3 7 + 5 = **15**	10. 4 2 + 8 = **14**	11. 1 1 + 5 = **7**	12. 4 0 + 6 = **10**
13. 2 2 + 5 = **9**	14. 3 5 + 6 = **14**	15. 5 1 + 6 = **12**	16. 11 8 + 8 = **27**	17. 4 8 + 4 = **16**	18. 5 7 + 4 = **16**
19. 3 9 + 3 = **15**	20. 1 3 + 8 = **12**	21. 7 1 + 5 = **13**	22. 12 0 + 6 = **18**	23. 5 4 + 7 = **16**	24. 3 0 + 8 = **11**
25. 4 8 + 5 = **17**	26. 9 3 + 3 = **15**	27. 10 0 + 8 = **18**			

72   CD-104318 • © Carson-Dellosa

Name _____ Date _____

Two-Digit Addition

Total Problems: **27**
Problems Correct: _____

Solve each problem.

Jump to It!

1. 45 + 30 = **75**	2. 37 + 22 = **59**	3. 37 + 30 = **67**	4. 47 + 31 = **78**	5. 26 + 53 = **79**	6. 52 + 42 = **94**
7. 14 + 34 = **48**	8. 13 + 43 = **56**	9. 32 + 51 = **83**	10. 28 + 51 = **79**	11. 36 + 41 = **77**	12. 65 + 34 = **99**
13. 72 + 12 = **84**	14. 44 + 25 = **69**	15. 55 + 22 = **77**	16. 62 + 34 = **96**	17. 64 + 25 = **89**	18. 75 + 24 = **99**
19. 23 + 14 = **37**	20. 16 + 60 = **76**	21. 75 + 24 = **99**	22. 37 + 51 = **88**	23. 32 + 47 = **79**	24. 31 + 48 = **79**
25. 61 + 26 = **87**	26. 44 + 32 = **76**	27. 35 + 44 = **79**			

CD-104318 • © Carson-Dellosa   73

Name _____ Date _____

Two-Digit Addition

Total Problems: **27**
Problems Correct: _____

Solve each problem.

Think Big!

1. 24 + 24 = **48**	2. 24 + 23 = **47**	3. 45 + 30 = **75**	4. 25 + 61 = **86**	5. 10 + 50 = **60**	6. 40 + 40 = **80**
7. 70 + 18 = **88**	8. 42 + 17 = **59**	9. 60 + 20 = **80**	10. 61 + 27 = **88**	11. 30 + 40 = **70**	12. 24 + 44 = **68**
13. 11 + 75 = **86**	14. 14 + 24 = **38**	15. 24 + 35 = **59**	16. 34 + 12 = **46**	17. 54 + 13 = **67**	18. 23 + 44 = **67**
19. 46 + 53 = **99**	20. 35 + 13 = **48**	21. 35 + 34 = **69**	22. 32 + 26 = **58**	23. 33 + 42 = **75**	24. 21 + 52 = **73**
25. 23 + 52 = **75**	26. 72 + 14 = **86**	27. 53 + 23 = **76**			

74   CD-104318 • © Carson-Dellosa

Name _____ Date _____

Two-Digit Addition

Total Problems: **27**
Problems Correct: _____

Solve each problem.

A Smile Is Key!

1. 27 + 82 = **109**	2. 74 + 95 = **169**	3. 80 + 60 = **140**	4. 95 + 44 = **139**	5. 94 + 93 = **187**	6. 41 + 75 = **116**
7. 82 + 71 = **153**	8. 97 + 81 = **178**	9. 85 + 91 = **176**	10. 33 + 85 = **118**	11. 92 + 54 = **146**	12. 74 + 80 = **154**
13. 11 + 75 = **86**	14. 53 + 72 = **125**	15. 83 + 84 = **167**	16. 52 + 85 = **137**	17. 65 + 42 = **107**	18. 94 + 64 = **158**
19. 72 + 72 = **144**	20. 95 + 33 = **128**	21. 44 + 92 = **136**	22. 52 + 56 = **108**	23. 71 + 66 = **137**	24. 60 + 85 = **145**
25. 93 + 26 = **119**	26. 32 + 72 = **104**	27. 44 + 84 = **128**			

CD-104318 • © Carson-Dellosa   75

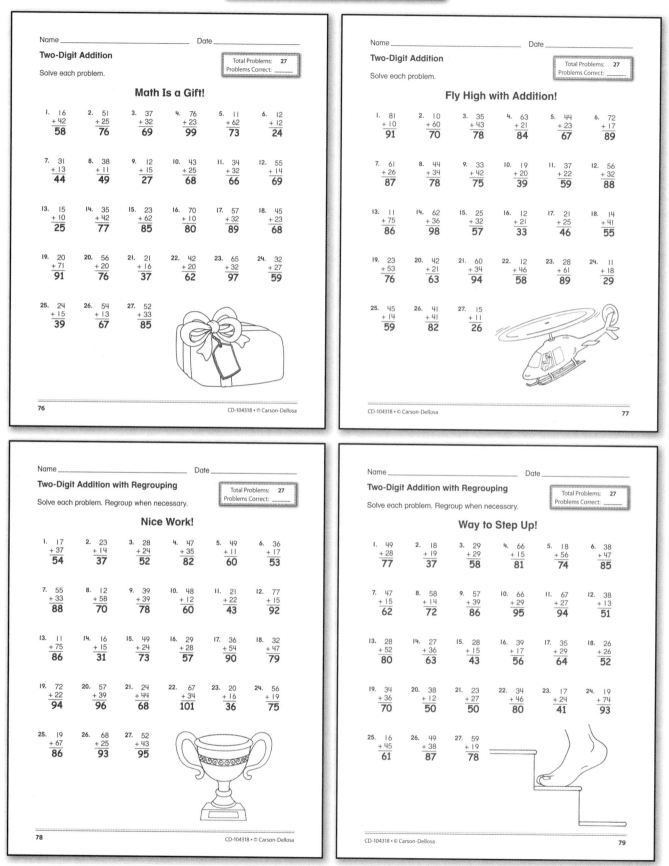

Worksheet 1 (page 76)

Name _____ Date _____

Two-Digit Addition

| Total Problems: 27 |
| Problems Correct: _____ |

Solve each problem.

Math Is a Gift!

1. 16 + 42 = 58
2. 51 + 25 = 76
3. 37 + 32 = 69
4. 76 + 23 = 99
5. 11 + 62 = 73
6. 12 + 12 = 24

7. 31 + 13 = 44
8. 38 + 11 = 49
9. 12 + 15 = 27
10. 43 + 25 = 68
11. 34 + 32 = 66
12. 55 + 14 = 69

13. 15 + 10 = 25
14. 35 + 42 = 77
15. 23 + 62 = 85
16. 70 + 10 = 80
17. 57 + 32 = 89
18. 45 + 23 = 68

19. 20 + 71 = 91
20. 56 + 20 = 76
21. 21 + 16 = 37
22. 42 + 20 = 62
23. 65 + 32 = 97
24. 32 + 27 = 59

25. 24 + 15 = 39
26. 54 + 13 = 67
27. 52 + 33 = 85

76 — CD-104318 • © Carson-Dellosa

Worksheet 2 (page 77)

Name _____ Date _____

Two-Digit Addition

| Total Problems: 27 |
| Problems Correct: _____ |

Solve each problem.

Fly High with Addition!

1. 81 + 10 = 91
2. 10 + 60 = 70
3. 35 + 43 = 78
4. 63 + 21 = 84
5. 44 + 23 = 67
6. 72 + 17 = 89

7. 61 + 26 = 87
8. 44 + 34 = 78
9. 33 + 42 = 75
10. 19 + 20 = 39
11. 37 + 22 = 59
12. 56 + 32 = 88

13. 11 + 75 = 86
14. 62 + 36 = 98
15. 25 + 32 = 57
16. 12 + 21 = 33
17. 21 + 25 = 46
18. 14 + 41 = 55

19. 23 + 53 = 76
20. 42 + 21 = 63
21. 60 + 34 = 94
22. 12 + 46 = 58
23. 28 + 61 = 89
24. 11 + 18 = 29

25. 45 + 14 = 59
26. 41 + 41 = 82
27. 15 + 11 = 26

CD-104318 • © Carson-Dellosa — 77

Worksheet 3 (page 78)

Name _____ Date _____

Two-Digit Addition with Regrouping

| Total Problems: 27 |
| Problems Correct: _____ |

Solve each problem. Regroup when necessary.

Nice Work!

1. 17 + 37 = 54
2. 23 + 14 = 37
3. 28 + 24 = 52
4. 47 + 35 = 82
5. 49 + 11 = 60
6. 36 + 17 = 53

7. 55 + 33 = 88
8. 12 + 58 = 70
9. 39 + 39 = 78
10. 48 + 12 = 60
11. 21 + 22 = 43
12. 77 + 15 = 92

13. 11 + 75 = 86
14. 16 + 15 = 31
15. 49 + 24 = 73
16. 29 + 28 = 57
17. 36 + 54 = 90
18. 32 + 47 = 79

19. 72 + 22 = 94
20. 57 + 39 = 96
21. 24 + 44 = 68
22. 67 + 34 = 101
23. 20 + 16 = 36
24. 56 + 19 = 75

25. 19 + 67 = 86
26. 68 + 25 = 93
27. 52 + 43 = 95

78 — CD-104318 • © Carson-Dellosa

Worksheet 4 (page 79)

Name _____ Date _____

Two-Digit Addition with Regrouping

| Total Problems: 27 |
| Problems Correct: _____ |

Solve each problem. Regroup when necessary.

Way to Step Up!

1. 49 + 28 = 77
2. 18 + 19 = 37
3. 29 + 29 = 58
4. 66 + 15 = 81
5. 18 + 56 = 74
6. 38 + 47 = 85

7. 47 + 15 = 62
8. 58 + 14 = 72
9. 57 + 39 = 86
10. 66 + 29 = 95
11. 67 + 27 = 94
12. 38 + 13 = 51

13. 28 + 52 = 80
14. 27 + 36 = 63
15. 28 + 15 = 43
16. 39 + 17 = 56
17. 35 + 29 = 64
18. 26 + 26 = 52

19. 34 + 36 = 70
20. 38 + 12 = 50
21. 23 + 27 = 50
22. 34 + 46 = 80
23. 17 + 24 = 41
24. 19 + 74 = 93

25. 16 + 45 = 61
26. 49 + 38 = 87
27. 59 + 19 = 78

CD-104318 • © Carson-Dellosa — 79

Answer Key

Name _____ Date _____

Two-Digit Addition with Regrouping

Total Problems: **27**
Problems Correct: _____

Solve each problem. Regroup when necessary.

Math Is a Treasure!

1. 13 + 28 = **41**	2. 66 + 27 = **93**	3. 67 + 18 = **85**	4. 39 + 14 = **53**	5. 26 + 59 = **85**	6. 22 + 18 = **40**
7. 65 + 26 = **91**	8. 45 + 19 = **64**	9. 55 + 37 = **92**	10. 16 + 16 = **32**	11. 39 + 38 = **77**	12. 52 + 28 = **80**
13. 44 + 39 = **83**	14. 42 + 29 = **71**	15. 15 + 28 = **43**	16. 29 + 23 = **52**	17. 14 + 49 = **63**	18. 48 + 27 = **75**
19. 37 + 17 = **54**	20. 27 + 19 = **46**	21. 21 + 39 = **60**	22. 32 + 39 = **71**	23. 22 + 28 = **50**	24. 78 + 19 = **97**
25. 38 + 36 = **74**	26. 18 + 18 = **36**	27. 24 + 56 = **80**			

CD-104318 • © Carson-Dellosa

Name _____ Date _____

Two-Digit Addition with Regrouping

Total Problems: **27**
Problems Correct: _____

Solve each problem. Regroup when necessary.

Munch on These Numbers!

1. 16 + 45 = **61**	2. 23 + 27 = **50**	3. 39 + 17 = **56**	4. 67 + 27 = **94**	5. 38 + 13 = **51**	6. 29 + 29 = **58**
7. 19 + 74 = **93**	8. 27 + 36 = **63**	9. 57 + 37 = **94**	10. 18 + 16 = **34**	11. 49 + 52 = **101**	12. 66 + 77 = **143**
13. 32 + 99 = **131**	14. 81 + 89 = **170**	15. 15 + 44 = **59**	16. 65 + 78 = **143**	17. 15 + 29 = **44**	18. 74 + 55 = **129**
19. 21 + 63 = **84**	20. 46 + 98 = **144**	21. 55 + 39 = **94**	22. 45 + 37 = **82**	23. 31 + 56 = **87**	24. 79 + 59 = **138**
25. 28 + 19 = **47**	26. 17 + 13 = **30**	27. 56 + 56 = **112**			

CD-104318 • © Carson-Dellosa

Name _____ Date _____

Two-Digit Subtraction

Total Problems: **27**
Problems Correct: _____

Solve each problem.

Keep Rolling Along!

1. 63 − 40 = **23**	2. 80 − 50 = **30**	3. 75 − 52 = **23**	4. 79 − 22 = **57**	5. 38 − 15 = **23**	6. 93 − 33 = **60**
7. 67 − 46 = **21**	8. 83 − 42 = **41**	9. 77 − 11 = **66**	10. 76 − 51 = **25**	11. 59 − 37 = **22**	12. 77 − 64 = **13**
13. 56 − 36 = **20**	14. 63 − 31 = **32**	15. 48 − 26 = **22**	16. 86 − 55 = **31**	17. 40 − 20 = **20**	18. 43 − 40 = **3**
19. 87 − 35 = **52**	20. 84 − 51 = **33**	21. 15 − 10 = **5**	22. 31 − 10 = **21**	23. 77 − 34 = **43**	24. 42 − 10 = **32**
25. 64 − 30 = **34**	26. 39 − 25 = **14**	27. 87 − 12 = **75**			

CD-104318 • © Carson-Dellosa

Name _____ Date _____

Two-Digit Subtraction

Total Problems: **27**
Problems Correct: _____

Solve each problem.

Use Your Subtraction Tools!

1. 61 − 41 = **20**	2. 39 − 26 = **13**	3. 85 − 43 = **42**	4. 56 − 31 = **25**	5. 47 − 17 = **30**	6. 87 − 45 = **42**
7. 67 − 52 = **15**	8. 78 − 33 = **45**	9. 69 − 46 = **23**	10. 96 − 21 = **75**	11. 94 − 71 = **23**	12. 40 − 20 = **20**
13. 70 − 20 = **50**	14. 98 − 31 = **67**	15. 58 − 18 = **40**	16. 38 − 15 = **23**	17. 65 − 12 = **53**	18. 88 − 62 = **26**
19. 26 − 24 = **2**	20. 70 − 20 = **50**	21. 82 − 51 = **31**	22. 62 − 20 = **42**	23. 98 − 34 = **64**	24. 88 − 12 = **76**
25. 45 − 35 = **10**	26. 67 − 45 = **22**	27. 19 − 15 = **4**			

CD-104318 • © Carson-Dellosa

Answer Key

Two-Digit Subtraction

Name _____ Date _____

Solve each problem.

Total Problems: **27**
Problems Correct: _____

Double the Fun!

1. 77 − 44 = 33
2. 55 − 22 = 33
3. 98 − 53 = 45
4. 29 − 14 = 15
5. 60 − 50 = 10
6. 69 − 22 = 47

7. 45 − 25 = 20
8. 78 − 61 = 17
9. 86 − 82 = 4
10. 39 − 13 = 26
11. 86 − 24 = 62
12. 59 − 51 = 8

13. 72 − 31 = 41
14. 93 − 81 = 12
15. 26 − 11 = 15
16. 98 − 14 = 84
17. 67 − 32 = 35
18. 39 − 13 = 26

19. 77 − 10 = 67
20. 87 − 15 = 72
21. 63 − 30 = 33
22. 82 − 71 = 11
23. 74 − 53 = 21
24. 83 − 42 = 41

25. 48 − 26 = 22
26. 82 − 22 = 60
27. 88 − 24 = 64

Two-Digit Subtraction

Name _____ Date _____

Solve each problem.

Total Problems: **27**
Problems Correct: _____

Now You're Soaring!

1. 56 − 21 = 35
2. 87 − 45 = 42
3. 68 − 36 = 32
4. 45 − 23 = 22
5. 87 − 34 = 53
6. 99 − 66 = 33

7. 76 − 75 = 1
8. 48 − 22 = 26
9. 29 − 12 = 17
10. 33 − 11 = 22
11. 67 − 34 = 33
12. 28 − 17 = 11

13. 65 − 32 = 33
14. 95 − 14 = 81
15. 82 − 22 = 60
16. 27 − 16 = 11
17. 69 − 34 = 35
18. 59 − 41 = 18

19. 74 − 22 = 52
20. 78 − 45 = 33
21. 89 − 88 = 1
22. 68 − 46 = 22
23. 39 − 22 = 17
24. 61 − 40 = 21

25. 56 − 23 = 33
26. 36 − 25 = 11
27. 77 − 66 = 11

Two-Digit Subtraction with Regrouping

Name _____ Date _____

Solve each problem. Regroup when necessary.

Total Problems: **27**
Problems Correct: _____

Take Your Time!

1. 61 − 29 = 32
2. 91 − 49 = 42
3. 66 − 18 = 48
4. 78 − 54 = 24
5. 31 − 15 = 16
6. 73 − 57 = 16

7. 40 − 23 = 17
8. 51 − 42 = 9
9. 77 − 23 = 54
10. 87 − 58 = 29
11. 96 − 45 = 51
12. 34 − 27 = 7

13. 85 − 36 = 49
14. 50 − 25 = 25
15. 26 − 11 = 15
16. 63 − 24 = 39
17. 86 − 69 = 17
18. 98 − 39 = 59

19. 97 − 48 = 49
20. 96 − 32 = 64
21. 79 − 56 = 23
22. 53 − 28 = 25
23. 24 − 17 = 7
24. 52 − 44 = 8

25. 43 − 18 = 25
26. 54 − 32 = 22
27. 41 − 28 = 13

Two-Digit Subtraction with Regrouping

Name _____ Date _____

Solve each problem. Regroup when necessary.

Total Problems: **27**
Problems Correct: _____

Take It Slow and Easy!

1. 26 − 18 = 8
2. 54 − 46 = 8
3. 42 − 33 = 9
4. 28 − 19 = 9
5. 53 − 46 = 7
6. 91 − 24 = 67

7. 65 − 46 = 19
8. 57 − 48 = 9
9. 81 − 72 = 9
10. 73 − 64 = 9
11. 26 − 18 = 8
12. 62 − 49 = 13

13. 60 − 37 = 23
14. 67 − 49 = 18
15. 52 − 43 = 9
16. 42 − 33 = 9
17. 55 − 47 = 8
18. 33 − 26 = 7

19. 34 − 27 = 7
20. 77 − 68 = 9
21. 67 − 19 = 48
22. 67 − 59 = 8
23. 82 − 45 = 37
24. 82 − 73 = 9

25. 31 − 19 = 12
26. 56 − 47 = 9
27. 48 − 39 = 9

Answer Key

Two-Digit Subtraction with Regrouping

Solve each problem. Regroup when necessary.

Total Problems: **27**
Problems Correct: _____

One Step at a Time!

1. $\begin{array}{r}26\\-19\\\hline 7\end{array}$	2. $\begin{array}{r}37\\-18\\\hline 19\end{array}$	3. $\begin{array}{r}98\\-49\\\hline 49\end{array}$	4. $\begin{array}{r}94\\-25\\\hline 69\end{array}$	5. $\begin{array}{r}66\\-48\\\hline 18\end{array}$	6. $\begin{array}{r}76\\-28\\\hline 48\end{array}$
7. $\begin{array}{r}34\\-17\\\hline 17\end{array}$	8. $\begin{array}{r}52\\-23\\\hline 29\end{array}$	9. $\begin{array}{r}31\\-27\\\hline 4\end{array}$	10. $\begin{array}{r}80\\-38\\\hline 42\end{array}$	11. $\begin{array}{r}86\\-47\\\hline 39\end{array}$	12. $\begin{array}{r}37\\-28\\\hline 9\end{array}$
13. $\begin{array}{r}63\\-26\\\hline 37\end{array}$	14. $\begin{array}{r}80\\-12\\\hline 68\end{array}$	15. $\begin{array}{r}97\\-69\\\hline 28\end{array}$	16. $\begin{array}{r}93\\-28\\\hline 65\end{array}$	17. $\begin{array}{r}83\\-57\\\hline 26\end{array}$	18. $\begin{array}{r}71\\-16\\\hline 55\end{array}$
19. $\begin{array}{r}40\\-38\\\hline 2\end{array}$	20. $\begin{array}{r}71\\-33\\\hline 38\end{array}$	21. $\begin{array}{r}55\\-27\\\hline 28\end{array}$	22. $\begin{array}{r}94\\-35\\\hline 59\end{array}$	23. $\begin{array}{r}78\\-49\\\hline 29\end{array}$	24. $\begin{array}{r}80\\-35\\\hline 45\end{array}$
25. $\begin{array}{r}43\\-38\\\hline 5\end{array}$	26. $\begin{array}{r}82\\-37\\\hline 45\end{array}$	27. $\begin{array}{r}81\\-24\\\hline 57\end{array}$			

Two-Digit Subtraction with Regrouping

Solve each problem. Regroup when necessary.

Total Problems: **27**
Problems Correct: _____

Practice, Practice, Practice!

1. $\begin{array}{r}40\\-19\\\hline 21\end{array}$	2. $\begin{array}{r}75\\-23\\\hline 52\end{array}$	3. $\begin{array}{r}62\\-48\\\hline 14\end{array}$	4. $\begin{array}{r}79\\-73\\\hline 6\end{array}$	5. $\begin{array}{r}66\\-29\\\hline 37\end{array}$	6. $\begin{array}{r}90\\-11\\\hline 79\end{array}$
7. $\begin{array}{r}91\\-35\\\hline 56\end{array}$	8. $\begin{array}{r}56\\-27\\\hline 29\end{array}$	9. $\begin{array}{r}91\\-42\\\hline 49\end{array}$	10. $\begin{array}{r}98\\-41\\\hline 57\end{array}$	11. $\begin{array}{r}41\\-20\\\hline 21\end{array}$	12. $\begin{array}{r}94\\-86\\\hline 8\end{array}$
13. $\begin{array}{r}86\\-21\\\hline 65\end{array}$	14. $\begin{array}{r}28\\-18\\\hline 10\end{array}$	15. $\begin{array}{r}64\\-58\\\hline 6\end{array}$	16. $\begin{array}{r}84\\-25\\\hline 59\end{array}$	17. $\begin{array}{r}60\\-20\\\hline 40\end{array}$	18. $\begin{array}{r}49\\-37\\\hline 12\end{array}$
19. $\begin{array}{r}94\\-66\\\hline 28\end{array}$	20. $\begin{array}{r}68\\-33\\\hline 35\end{array}$	21. $\begin{array}{r}61\\-37\\\hline 24\end{array}$	22. $\begin{array}{r}52\\-33\\\hline 19\end{array}$	23. $\begin{array}{r}97\\-49\\\hline 48\end{array}$	24. $\begin{array}{r}46\\-12\\\hline 34\end{array}$
25. $\begin{array}{r}29\\-17\\\hline 12\end{array}$	26. $\begin{array}{r}63\\-40\\\hline 23\end{array}$	27. $\begin{array}{r}78\\-35\\\hline 43\end{array}$			

Two-Digit Subtraction with Regrouping

Solve each problem. Regroup when necessary.

Total Problems: **27**
Problems Correct: _____

You're Out of This World!

1. $\begin{array}{r}73\\-22\\\hline 51\end{array}$	2. $\begin{array}{r}80\\-14\\\hline 66\end{array}$	3. $\begin{array}{r}66\\-28\\\hline 38\end{array}$	4. $\begin{array}{r}46\\-35\\\hline 11\end{array}$	5. $\begin{array}{r}26\\-18\\\hline 8\end{array}$	6. $\begin{array}{r}87\\-38\\\hline 49\end{array}$
7. $\begin{array}{r}63\\-36\\\hline 27\end{array}$	8. $\begin{array}{r}52\\-28\\\hline 24\end{array}$	9. $\begin{array}{r}97\\-63\\\hline 34\end{array}$	10. $\begin{array}{r}34\\-27\\\hline 7\end{array}$	11. $\begin{array}{r}77\\-57\\\hline 20\end{array}$	12. $\begin{array}{r}34\\-29\\\hline 5\end{array}$
13. $\begin{array}{r}71\\-35\\\hline 36\end{array}$	14. $\begin{array}{r}35\\-26\\\hline 9\end{array}$	15. $\begin{array}{r}99\\-12\\\hline 87\end{array}$	16. $\begin{array}{r}53\\-44\\\hline 9\end{array}$	17. $\begin{array}{r}90\\-33\\\hline 57\end{array}$	18. $\begin{array}{r}93\\-15\\\hline 78\end{array}$
19. $\begin{array}{r}90\\-12\\\hline 78\end{array}$	20. $\begin{array}{r}82\\-39\\\hline 43\end{array}$	21. $\begin{array}{r}83\\-39\\\hline 44\end{array}$	22. $\begin{array}{r}43\\-12\\\hline 31\end{array}$	23. $\begin{array}{r}72\\-43\\\hline 29\end{array}$	24. $\begin{array}{r}57\\-48\\\hline 9\end{array}$
25. $\begin{array}{r}82\\-49\\\hline 33\end{array}$	26. $\begin{array}{r}78\\-65\\\hline 13\end{array}$	27. $\begin{array}{r}66\\-55\\\hline 11\end{array}$			

Two-Digit Addition and Subtraction

Solve each problem.

Total Problems: **27**
Problems Correct: _____

Going Up and Down!

1. $\begin{array}{r}74\\-30\\\hline 44\end{array}$	2. $\begin{array}{r}76\\+22\\\hline 98\end{array}$	3. $\begin{array}{r}72\\+23\\\hline 95\end{array}$	4. $\begin{array}{r}74\\+12\\\hline 86\end{array}$	5. $\begin{array}{r}85\\-61\\\hline 24\end{array}$	6. $\begin{array}{r}45\\+24\\\hline 69\end{array}$
7. $\begin{array}{r}60\\+34\\\hline 94\end{array}$	8. $\begin{array}{r}78\\+21\\\hline 99\end{array}$	9. $\begin{array}{r}76\\-26\\\hline 50\end{array}$	10. $\begin{array}{r}43\\-23\\\hline 20\end{array}$	11. $\begin{array}{r}78\\-21\\\hline 57\end{array}$	12. $\begin{array}{r}43\\+53\\\hline 96\end{array}$
13. $\begin{array}{r}16\\+12\\\hline 28\end{array}$	14. $\begin{array}{r}54\\-32\\\hline 22\end{array}$	15. $\begin{array}{r}82\\-42\\\hline 40\end{array}$	16. $\begin{array}{r}33\\+33\\\hline 66\end{array}$	17. $\begin{array}{r}75\\+24\\\hline 99\end{array}$	18. $\begin{array}{r}64\\-23\\\hline 41\end{array}$
19. $\begin{array}{r}45\\-21\\\hline 24\end{array}$	20. $\begin{array}{r}76\\-25\\\hline 51\end{array}$	21. $\begin{array}{r}54\\+45\\\hline 99\end{array}$	22. $\begin{array}{r}67\\+22\\\hline 89\end{array}$	23. $\begin{array}{r}66\\-51\\\hline 15\end{array}$	24. $\begin{array}{r}83\\-62\\\hline 21\end{array}$
25. $\begin{array}{r}52\\-31\\\hline 21\end{array}$	26. $\begin{array}{r}34\\+22\\\hline 56\end{array}$	27. $\begin{array}{r}43\\+34\\\hline 77\end{array}$			

Name _____ Date _____

Two-Digit Addition and Subtraction

Solve each problem.

Total Problems: 27
Problems Correct: _____

Stepping Up to the Plate!

1. 77 − 63 = **14**	2. 17 + 40 = **57**	3. 44 + 22 = **66**	4. 76 + 23 = **99**	5. 86 − 44 = **42**	6. 42 + 34 = **76**
7. 27 + 31 = **58**	8. 55 + 42 = **97**	9. 77 − 36 = **41**	10. 47 − 26 = **21**	11. 24 + 34 = **58**	12. 78 + 21 = **99**
13. 95 − 30 = **65**	14. 95 − 50 = **45**	15. 75 − 30 = **45**	16. 72 + 21 = **93**	17. 62 + 36 = **98**	18. 57 − 16 = **41**
19. 57 − 57 = **0**	20. 36 − 15 = **21**	21. 61 + 33 = **94**	22. 43 + 23 = **66**	23. 83 − 20 = **63**	24. 89 − 61 = **28**
25. 69 − 51 = **18**	26. 38 + 40 = **78**	27. 75 + 21 = **96**			

92   CD-104318 • © Carson-Dellosa

Name _____ Date _____

Two-Digit Addition and Subtraction with Regrouping

Solve each problem. Regroup when necessary.

Total Problems: 27
Problems Correct: _____

Let's Get Rolling!

1. 32 − 16 = **16**	2. 41 + 49 = **90**	3. 67 + 28 = **95**	4. 37 + 37 = **74**	5. 59 − 44 = **15**	6. 45 + 56 = **101**
7. 40 + 63 = **103**	8. 78 + 46 = **124**	9. 70 − 10 = **60**	10. 73 − 63 = **10**	11. 64 + 71 = **135**	12. 90 + 34 = **124**
13. 66 − 30 = **36**	14. 67 − 49 = **18**	15. 92 − 57 = **35**	16. 45 + 89 = **134**	17. 32 + 32 = **64**	18. 88 − 64 = **24**
19. 95 − 52 = **43**	20. 79 − 26 = **53**	21. 23 + 41 = **64**	22. 82 + 53 = **135**	23. 90 − 25 = **65**	24. 73 − 41 = **32**
25. 98 − 21 = **77**	26. 31 + 29 = **60**	27. 76 + 47 = **123**			

CD-104318 • © Carson-Dellosa   93

Name _____ Date _____

Two- and Three-Digit Addition

Solve each problem.

Total Problems: 27
Problems Correct: _____

Addition Is a Walk in the Park!

1. 12 + 45 = **57**	2. 44 + 35 = **79**	3. 43 + 21 = **64**	4. 70 + 29 = **99**	5. 43 + 26 = **69**	6. 440 + 150 = **590**
7. 982 + 12 = **994**	8. 323 + 433 = **756**	9. 609 + 290 = **899**	10. 44 + 22 = **66**	11. 137 + 122 = **259**	12. 251 + 540 = **791**
13. 200 + 400 = **600**	14. 521 + 342 = **863**	15. 601 + 216 = **817**	16. 175 + 22 = **197**	17. 113 + 305 = **418**	18. 181 + 14 = **195**
19. 342 + 50 = **392**	20. 576 + 103 = **679**	21. 700 + 43 = **743**	22. 645 + 223 = **868**	23. 73 + 23 = **96**	24. 121 + 131 = **252**
25. 70 + 20 = **90**	26. 443 + 53 = **496**	27. 835 + 124 = **959**			

94   CD-104318 • © Carson-Dellosa

Name _____ Date _____

Three-Digit Addition

Solve each problem.

Total Problems: 27
Problems Correct: _____

Go for It!

1. 486 + 313 = **799**	2. 639 + 250 = **889**	3. 387 + 412 = **799**	4. 563 + 416 = **979**	5. 574 + 225 = **799**	6. 362 + 332 = **694**
7. 667 + 300 = **967**	8. 450 + 246 = **696**	9. 738 + 261 = **999**	10. 113 + 215 = **328**	11. 532 + 213 = **745**	12. 561 + 238 = **799**
13. 342 + 237 = **579**	14. 674 + 225 = **899**	15. 437 + 152 = **589**	16. 768 + 221 = **989**	17. 342 + 321 = **663**	18. 785 + 113 = **898**
19. 834 + 165 = **999**	20. 652 + 234 = **886**	21. 460 + 339 = **799**	22. 437 + 232 = **669**	23. 434 + 432 = **866**	24. 674 + 225 = **899**
25. 856 + 143 = **999**	26. 656 + 223 = **879**	27. 435 + 264 = **699**			

CD-104318 • © Carson-Dellosa   95

Answer Key

Page 96

Name _____ Date _____

Two- and Three-Digit Subtraction

Solve each problem.

Total Problems: 27
Problems Correct: _____

Take a Shot!

1. 65 − 33 = 32
2. 99 − 45 = 54
3. 89 − 56 = 33
4. 86 − 23 = 63
5. 379 − 163 = 216
6. 977 − 431 = 546

7. 795 − 461 = 334
8. 785 − 243 = 542
9. 196 − 81 = 115
10. 899 − 276 = 623
11. 439 − 121 = 318
12. 769 − 342 = 427

13. 98 − 46 = 52
14. 998 − 354 = 644
15. 143 − 33 = 110
16. 978 − 453 = 525
17. 398 − 346 = 52
18. 300 − 200 = 100

19. 925 − 14 = 911
20. 170 − 130 = 40
21. 286 − 166 = 120
22. 487 − 267 = 220
23. 364 − 50 = 314
24. 856 − 113 = 743

25. 886 − 332 = 554
26. 934 − 211 = 723
27. 378 − 245 = 133

96   CD-104318 • © Carson-Dellosa

Page 97

Name _____ Date _____

Three-Digit Subtraction

Solve each problem.

Total Problems: 27
Problems Correct: _____

Yes, You Can!

1. 887 − 354 = 533
2. 427 − 211 = 216
3. 674 − 124 = 550
4. 675 − 243 = 432
5. 697 − 463 = 234
6. 715 − 704 = 11

7. 400 − 300 = 100
8. 856 − 431 = 425
9. 498 − 268 = 230
10. 397 − 231 = 166
11. 333 − 222 = 111
12. 745 − 312 = 433

13. 786 − 231 = 555
14. 869 − 341 = 528
15. 847 − 243 = 604
16. 879 − 239 = 640
17. 632 − 131 = 501
18. 678 − 132 = 546

19. 849 − 832 = 17
20. 770 − 340 = 430
21. 657 − 121 = 536
22. 387 − 132 = 255
23. 879 − 436 = 443
24. 418 − 317 = 101

25. 680 − 220 = 460
26. 834 − 212 = 622
27. 356 − 254 = 102

CD-104318 • © Carson-Dellosa   97

Page 98

Name _____ Date _____

Three-Digit Addition and Subtraction with Regrouping

Solve each problem. Regroup when necessary.

Total Problems: 27
Problems Correct: _____

Hang in There!

1. 539 − 375 = 164
2. 476 + 243 = 719
3. 176 + 484 = 660
4. 392 + 292 = 684
5. 787 − 598 = 189
6. 165 + 427 = 592

7. 481 + 428 = 909
8. 842 + 177 = 1,019
9. 762 − 395 = 367
10. 856 − 399 = 457
11. 347 + 983 = 1,330
12. 275 + 298 = 573

13. 628 − 137 = 491
14. 531 − 467 = 64
15. 496 − 288 = 208
16. 389 + 392 = 781
17. 276 + 391 = 667
18. 374 − 276 = 98

19. 983 − 468 = 515
20. 834 − 376 = 458
21. 452 + 287 = 739
22. 392 + 284 = 676
23. 597 − 388 = 209
24. 584 − 287 = 297

25. 498 − 269 = 229
26. 735 + 373 = 1,108
27. 392 + 161 = 553

98   CD-104318 • © Carson-Dellosa

Page 99

Name _____ Date _____

Multiplication with Factors 0 to 5

Solve each problem.

Total Problems: 27
Problems Correct: _____

Leaping into Multiplication!

1. 5 × 3 = 15
2. 3 × 4 = 12
3. 5 × 1 = 5
4. 2 × 3 = 6
5. 1 × 0 = 0
6. 5 × 5 = 25

7. 1 × 3 = 3
8. 2 × 0 = 0
9. 2 × 4 = 8
10. 2 × 3 = 6
11. 2 × 2 = 4
12. 4 × 5 = 20

13. 3 × 3 = 9
14. 4 × 3 = 12
15. 4 × 1 = 4
16. 3 × 0 = 0
17. 5 × 3 = 15
18. 2 × 0 = 0

19. 2 × 1 = 2
20. 1 × 5 = 5
21. 1 × 2 = 2
22. 1 × 0 = 0
23. 4 × 5 = 20
24. 1 × 4 = 4

25. 3 × 5 = 15
26. 5 × 2 = 10
27. 5 × 5 = 25

CD-104318 • © Carson-Dellosa   99

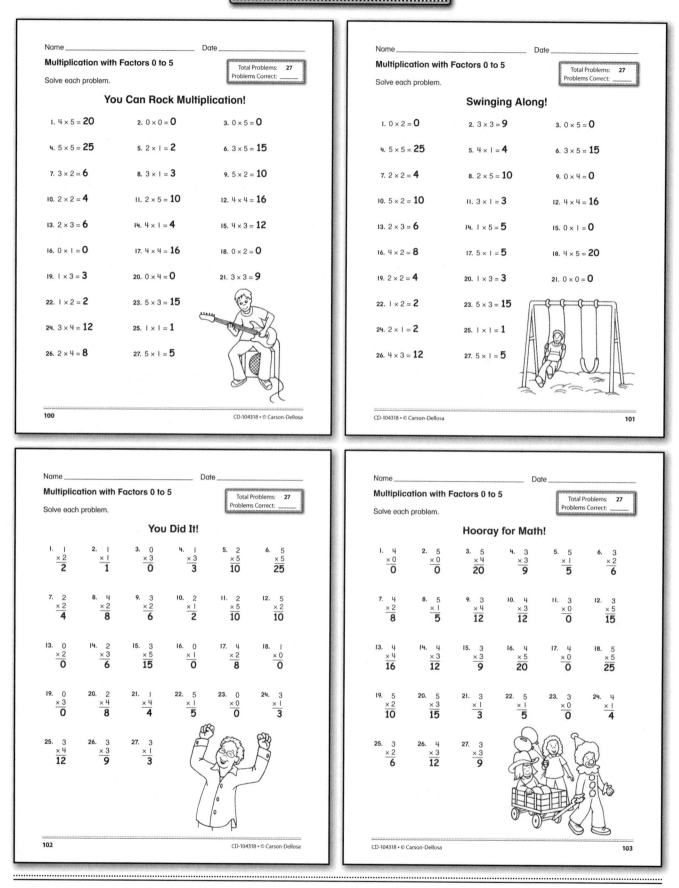

Name _____ Date _____

Multiplication with Factors 0 to 5

Solve each problem.

Total Problems: 27
Problems Correct: _____

You Can Rock Multiplication!

1. $4 \times 5 = 20$ 2. $0 \times 0 = 0$ 3. $0 \times 5 = 0$

4. $5 \times 5 = 25$ 5. $2 \times 1 = 2$ 6. $3 \times 5 = 15$

7. $3 \times 2 = 6$ 8. $3 \times 1 = 3$ 9. $5 \times 2 = 10$

10. $2 \times 2 = 4$ 11. $2 \times 5 = 10$ 12. $4 \times 4 = 16$

13. $2 \times 3 = 6$ 14. $4 \times 1 = 4$ 15. $4 \times 3 = 12$

16. $0 \times 1 = 0$ 17. $4 \times 4 = 16$ 18. $0 \times 2 = 0$

19. $1 \times 3 = 3$ 20. $0 \times 4 = 0$ 21. $3 \times 3 = 9$

22. $1 \times 2 = 2$ 23. $5 \times 3 = 15$

24. $3 \times 4 = 12$ 25. $1 \times 1 = 1$

26. $2 \times 4 = 8$ 27. $5 \times 1 = 5$

100 CD-104318 • © Carson-Dellosa

Name _____ Date _____

Multiplication with Factors 0 to 5

Solve each problem.

Total Problems: 27
Problems Correct: _____

Swinging Along!

1. $0 \times 2 = 0$ 2. $3 \times 3 = 9$ 3. $0 \times 5 = 0$

4. $5 \times 5 = 25$ 5. $4 \times 1 = 4$ 6. $3 \times 5 = 15$

7. $2 \times 2 = 4$ 8. $2 \times 5 = 10$ 9. $0 \times 4 = 0$

10. $5 \times 2 = 10$ 11. $3 \times 1 = 3$ 12. $4 \times 4 = 16$

13. $2 \times 3 = 6$ 14. $1 \times 5 = 5$ 15. $0 \times 1 = 0$

16. $4 \times 2 = 8$ 17. $5 \times 1 = 5$ 18. $4 \times 5 = 20$

19. $2 \times 2 = 4$ 20. $1 \times 3 = 3$ 21. $0 \times 0 = 0$

22. $1 \times 2 = 2$ 23. $5 \times 3 = 15$

24. $2 \times 1 = 2$ 25. $1 \times 1 = 1$

26. $4 \times 3 = 12$ 27. $5 \times 1 = 5$

CD-104318 • © Carson-Dellosa 101

Name _____ Date _____

Multiplication with Factors 0 to 5

Solve each problem.

Total Problems: 27
Problems Correct: _____

You Did It!

1. $1 \times 2 = 2$ 2. $1 \times 1 = 1$ 3. $0 \times 3 = 0$ 4. $1 \times 3 = 3$ 5. $2 \times 5 = 10$ 6. $5 \times 5 = 25$

7. $2 \times 2 = 4$ 8. $4 \times 2 = 8$ 9. $3 \times 2 = 6$ 10. $2 \times 1 = 2$ 11. $2 \times 5 = 10$ 12. $5 \times 2 = 10$

13. $0 \times 2 = 0$ 14. $2 \times 3 = 6$ 15. $3 \times 5 = 15$ 16. $0 \times 1 = 0$ 17. $4 \times 2 = 8$ 18. $1 \times 0 = 0$

19. $0 \times 3 = 0$ 20. $2 \times 4 = 8$ 21. $1 \times 4 = 4$ 22. $5 \times 1 = 5$ 23. $0 \times 0 = 0$ 24. $3 \times 1 = 3$

25. $3 \times 4 = 12$ 26. $3 \times 3 = 9$ 27. $3 \times 1 = 3$

102 CD-104318 • © Carson-Dellosa

Name _____ Date _____

Multiplication with Factors 0 to 5

Solve each problem.

Total Problems: 27
Problems Correct: _____

Hooray for Math!

1. $4 \times 0 = 0$ 2. $5 \times 0 = 0$ 3. $5 \times 4 = 20$ 4. $3 \times 3 = 9$ 5. $5 \times 1 = 5$ 6. $3 \times 2 = 6$

7. $4 \times 2 = 8$ 8. $5 \times 1 = 5$ 9. $3 \times 4 = 12$ 10. $4 \times 3 = 12$ 11. $3 \times 0 = 0$ 12. $3 \times 5 = 15$

13. $4 \times 4 = 16$ 14. $4 \times 3 = 12$ 15. $3 \times 3 = 9$ 16. $4 \times 5 = 20$ 17. $4 \times 0 = 0$ 18. $5 \times 5 = 25$

19. $5 \times 2 = 10$ 20. $5 \times 3 = 15$ 21. $3 \times 1 = 3$ 22. $5 \times 1 = 5$ 23. $3 \times 0 = 0$ 24. $4 \times 1 = 4$

25. $3 \times 2 = 6$ 26. $4 \times 3 = 12$ 27. $3 \times 3 = 9$

CD-104318 • © Carson-Dellosa 103

Congratulations!

receives this award for

Signed

Date

1 + 1	1 + 2	1 + 3	1 + 4
1 + 5	1 + 6	1 + 7	1 + 8
1 + 9	2 + 2	2 + 3	2 + 4
2 + 5	2 + 6	2 + 7	2 + 8

5   4   3   2

<u>9</u>   8   7   <u>6</u>

<u>6</u>   5   4   10

10   <u>9</u>   8   7

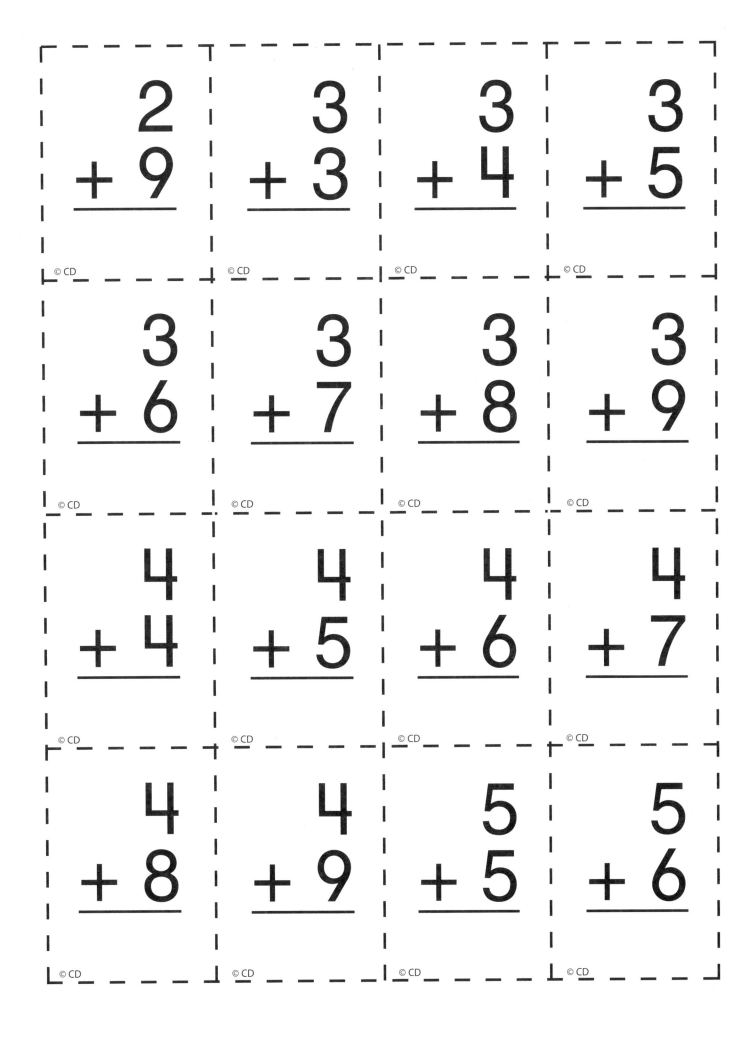

2	3	3	3
+ 9	+ 3	+ 4	+ 5
© CD	© CD	© CD	© CD
3	3	3	3
+ 6	+ 7	+ 8	+ 9
© CD	© CD	© CD	© CD
4	4	4	4
+ 4	+ 5	+ 6	+ 7
© CD	© CD	© CD	© CD
4	4	5	5
+ 8	+ 9	+ 5	+ 6
© CD	© CD	© CD	© CD

$\begin{array}{r} 5 \\ +\ 7 \\ \hline \end{array}$	$\begin{array}{r} 5 \\ +\ 8 \\ \hline \end{array}$	$\begin{array}{r} 5 \\ +\ 9 \\ \hline \end{array}$	$\begin{array}{r} 6 \\ +\ 6 \\ \hline \end{array}$
$\begin{array}{r} 6 \\ +\ 7 \\ \hline \end{array}$	$\begin{array}{r} 6 \\ +\ 8 \\ \hline \end{array}$	$\begin{array}{r} 6 \\ +\ 9 \\ \hline \end{array}$	$\begin{array}{r} 7 \\ +\ 7 \\ \hline \end{array}$
$\begin{array}{r} 7 \\ +\ 8 \\ \hline \end{array}$	$\begin{array}{r} 7 \\ +\ 9 \\ \hline \end{array}$	$\begin{array}{r} 8 \\ +\ 8 \\ \hline \end{array}$	$\begin{array}{r} 8 \\ +\ 9 \\ \hline \end{array}$
$\begin{array}{r} 9 \\ +\ 9 \\ \hline \end{array}$	$\begin{array}{r} 1 \\ -\ 1 \\ \hline \end{array}$	$\begin{array}{r} 2 \\ -\ 2 \\ \hline \end{array}$	$\begin{array}{r} 2 \\ -\ 1 \\ \hline \end{array}$

3 − 3	3 − 2	3 − 1	4 − 4
4 − 3	4 − 2	4 − 1	5 − 5
5 − 4	5 − 3	5 − 2	5 − 1
6 − 6	6 − 5	6 − 4	6 − 3

© CD

0   2   I   0

0   3   2   I

4   3   2   I

3   2   I   0

6 − 2	6 − 1	7 − 7	7 − 6
© CD	© CD	© CD	© CD
7 − 5	7 − 4	7 − 3	7 − 2
© CD	© CD	© CD	© CD
7 − 1	8 − 8	8 − 7	8 − 6
© CD	© CD	© CD	© CD
8 − 5	8 − 4	8 − 3	8 − 2
© CD	© CD	© CD	© CD

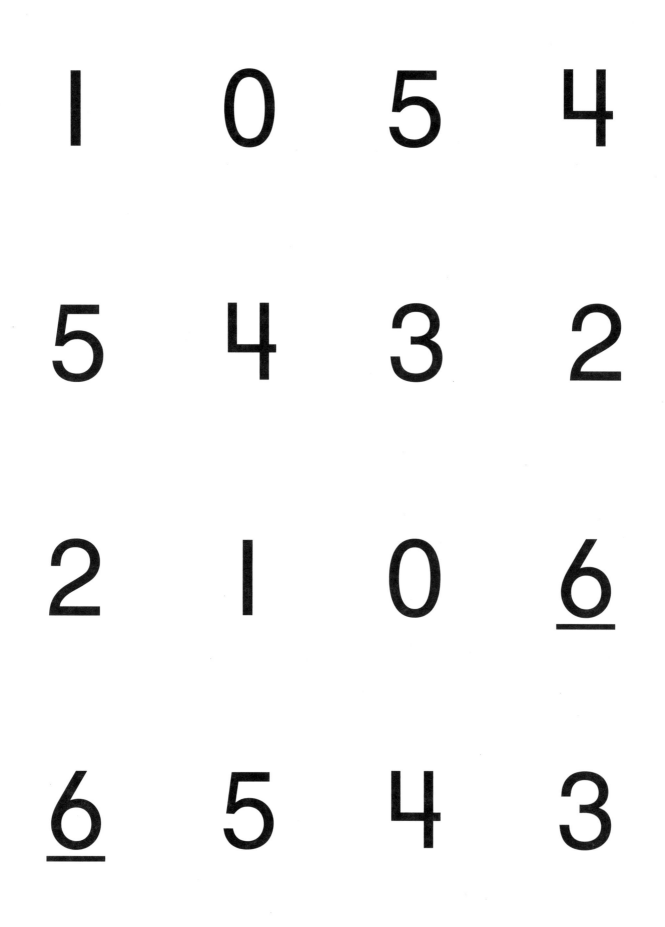

8 − 1	9 − 9	9 − 8	9 − 7
© CD	© CD	© CD	© CD
9 − 6	9 − 5	9 − 4	9 − 3
© CD	© CD	© CD	© CD
9 − 2	9 − 1	10 − 0	−
© CD	© CD	© CD	© CD
+	×	=	
© CD	© CD	© CD	

2   1   0   7

<u>6</u>   5   4   3

minus   10   8   7

equals   times   plus